WORLD INEQUALITIES

IN HUMAN DEVELOPMENT INDEX

(1980-2012)

PAVLE SICHERL

Gaptimer Report No. 1

Copyright © 2014 Pavle Sicherl

Ljubljana, January 2014

Layout and Figures: Jaka Hajnšek

Printed by CreateSpace, An Amazon.com Company.

ISBN 978-1495231896

FOREWORD

Inequalities in the world, between and within countries, are together with environment the critical issues for the 21st century. The Millennium Development Goals (MDGs) are coming towards conclusion and the international community is deciding on the scope and the timetable for a set of sustainable development goals (SDGs). There are a number of materials like UN (2013), Sustainable Development Solutions Network (2013), and OECD (2013) towards post-2015 agenda.

Better governance needs many things but also better data and tools for fact based decision making. The art of handling different views of data is crucial for discovering the relevant patterns and for providing a broader framework for policy and business analysis. Sustainable development is by definition a long-run and multi-dimensional phenomenon. Semantics of discussing the issues, in setting the targets and in the implementation should not be based only on static measures; it needs to be complemented by dynamic measures. Gaptimer Report No. 1 presents an innovation that goes beyond the present state-of-the art in measuring the degree of inequality thus increasing the understanding of the situation in the time perspective.

Seeing with new eyes creates new knowledge and better understanding. The relations between efficiency, growth, disparity, and equity are in this conceptual framework more pronounced than in the conventional analysis (Sicherl, 1992). A hypothesis can be formulated that, ceteris paribus, increased tensions may be partially a result of an increase in overall disparity through increased time distances brought about by lower growth rates.

Time distance methodology can be very helpful both in the preparation of the post-2015 agenda as well as in the continuous monitoring of implementation of selected indicators later, both on the aggregate and national levels. The first step in building any strategy is the assessment of the starting position. This report analyses it for the domain of the Human Development Index (HDI), it is applicable to indicators in other domains, including MDG.

The Guardian published on their Global development web site my article on time distance method of measuring implementation of MDGs, where Gaptimer progress chart summarised the situation over 7 world regions and 10 selected MDG indicators around 2010 (Sicherl, 2013a). Further analysis of the lessons of past implementation is expected to appear as one of the next volumes in the series Gaptimer Reports as further material for the post-2015 agenda. Potential users of this methodology could be international and national organizations, NGOs, experts, businesses, managers, educators, students, interest groups, media, and the general public at the world, national, and sub-national levels.

Ljubljana, January 2014   Pavle Sicherl

TABLE OF CONTENTS

FOREWORD   3

TABLE OF CONTENTS   5

Chapter 1 INTRODUCTION   7

Chapter 2 TIME DISTANCE PERSPECTIVE LOOKING AND SEEING WITH NEW EYES   9

Methodology: Time distance measure as additional perspective in measuring inequalities   9

Gender inequality in life expectancy – static distance and time distance   9

A brief definition of two novel statistical measures: S-time-distance and S-time-step   10

World inequalities in life expectancy at birth   11

Different perception of inequality based on percentage and time distance measures   15

Last but not least: S-time-step as an additional measure of dynamics   16

Methodological conclusions and results for health index   17

Chapter 3 TRENDS IN WORLD INEQUALITIES IN HUMAN DEVELOPMENT INDEX   19

Trends over the three decades for four human development groups in HDI, non-income HDI, and income index   19

Trends and S-time-distance for HDI for 13 selected countries over the range of all 187 countries   21

Chapter 4 OVERALL HUMAN DEVELOPMENT INDEX, HEALTH, EDUCATION, AND INCOME COMPONENTS   25

Comparisons of world inequalities over four HD groups and four indices (trends 1980-2012)   25

S-time-step as a measure of dynamics over all human development groups   27

Chapter 5 AN OVERVIEW OVER 187 COUNTRIES TIME DISTANCE INEQUALITIES WITHIN THE FOUR HUMAN DEVELOPMENT GROUPS   29

Time distance inequalities within the very high HD group   29

Time distance inequalities within the high HD group   30

Time distance inequalities within the medium HD group   31

Time distance inequalities within the low HD group   32

An overview of different perception of inequality based on percentage and time distance measures for HDI   33

Chapter 6 DISPARITIES WITHIN EU 27   37

Comparisons of S-time-distances for HDI for EU27 countries and average of the very high HD group   38

Comparing the HDI position of five Central European countries with very high HD group and among themselves   39

Chapter 7 BRICS COUNTRIES   **43**

Chapter 8 GULF COORDINATION COUNCIL COUNTRIES   **47**

Chapter 9 CONCLUSIONS   **49**

REFERENCES   **55**

LIST OF FIGURES AND TABLES   **57**

    Figures   57

    Tables   58

APPENDIX - ELECTRONIC SUPPLEMENTARY MATERIAL   **59**

    A1 Methodology   59

    A2 More detailed HDI time matrices and S-time-step calculations for 187 countries   60

INDEX   **61**

    Index for 187 Countries   61

ABOUT THE AUTHOR   **64**

Chapter 1

INTRODUCTION

The Human Development Index (HDI) published by UNDP is a composite indicator with well documented database and continuous improvements including additional disaggregations. HDI combines health index, education index, and income index and is a partial measure that attempts to provide a broad vision of the advance of countries in furthering capabilities. The degree of inequality between the four human development groups expressed in time distances shows that despite substantial progress inequalities remain very large.

At the 2013 Global Forum on Development at the OECD in the session 'Innovative approaches to measuring poverty, well-being and progress, and implications for statistical capacity development' organizers put the question how statisticians can take advantage of innovations in data production and dissemination. It is important to emphasise that in the chain of reasoning Statistics – Knowledge – Policy in addition to data and indicators we need also more work on measures and methods used to build perceptions about development and inequalities. This includes innovations in introducing new statistical measures that are transparent and easily understood by everyone in order to foster dissemination for policy use and to build transparency for broader participation of stakeholders. Measurement is costly and it is important how efficiently we exploit existing data for such purposes.

The time distance methodology applied to HDI opens new dynamic vistas of development and inequalities in the world. Empirically, when comparing across indicators and across time, static and time distance measures can give different perceptions of the order of magnitude of inequality within and between countries, so both dimensions matter. The published trends of the HDI and component indices (1980-2012) provide data that make it possible to combine the time distance methodology of measuring the degree of inequality with a well established international database and observe what additional new insights could be established with the novel method.

The applications of the time distance methodology fall in two main categories. The first is application in statistics, by adding two generic measures (S-time-distance and S-time-step) to the present state-of-the-art of measuring differences between time series that can be used both as descriptive tools and in analysis of goodness-of–fit; with possible further applications in other domains. On the scientific side, the fact that the Nobel Prize winner C. Granger extended the use of S-time-distance measure to econometric forecasting is an evidence of the generic capability of the idea.

The second application is for better understanding of the information embodied in time-series data to wider audiences, providing new perceptions for building knowledge and for discussing policy and business issues. The concept of time distance allows the second complementary dimension for comparison, visualisation and evaluations – in addition to the conventional static difference in levels for a given point in time the second dimension is the difference in time when the two compared units achieved the same level of the analysed indicator. Expressed in time units it is easily understandable to all, from policy makers, experts, and media to the general public. It also provides broader semantics for policy debate and management decisions as well as broader dynamic presentations of reality.

Sicherl (2011a) discusses the concept of 'overall degree of disparity', arguing that disparities in society depend not only on static measures of inequality but also on time distances. Further discussion on inter-temporal aspect of wellbeing will be available in Sicherl (in press). Such a broader concept of the overall degree of disparity can lead to a different perception of the extent of disparity than the conventional static measures alone.

Sicherl (2012) presents a simple example of comparing two countries or regions or social groups for a given indicator, assuming two scenarios. Scenario A assumes growth rate of 4%, and scenario B growth rate of 1%, for simplicity reasons both units are growing at these constant rates of growth. The value of the indicator for region 1 is 50% higher than that of region 2 in both scenarios. If one uses for the evaluation of the magnitude of the gap between the two regions the conventional statistical measures like ratio, percentage, Gini coefficient, Theil index, these two scenarios show the same degree of disparity. Taking the broader view of the situation (with the concept of time distance as one of the dimensions of disparity) this leads to a different conclusion about the degree of disparity in scenario A and in scenario B. In the 4% growth rate for scenario A with the 50% static disparity the time distance between the two compared units, countries, regions, or social groups is 10 years, in scenario B with 1% growth rate the time distance between the compared units is 40 years. It is highly unlikely that people would perceive such situations (combination static 50% and 10 years or static 50% and 40 years, respectively) as equal degrees of inequality as would be suggested by conventional static measures.

Chapter 2 presents the time distance methodology on the example of inequalities in life expectancy. The static difference in life expectancy for China against Sweden was less than 10 percent (which may appear to be small) while the time distance was about 50 years (which gives a very different perception of the magnitude of the gap). Chapters 3 and 4 analyse trends in HDI and its components over the three decades (1980-2012) for four human development groups. Chapter 5 presents S-time-distance estimates for HDI inequalities within the four groups for 187 countries. Chapters 6, 7, and 8 look at inequalities within EU27, BRICS countries, and Gulf Coordination Council countries, respectively. Conclusions and Appendix with electronic supplementary material on HDI for 187 countries follow.

Chapter 2

TIME DISTANCE PERSPECTIVE LOOKING AND SEEING WITH NEW EYES

Methodology: Time distance measure as additional perspective in measuring inequalities

Time distance is an innovative approach for looking at time-series data. Expressed in time units, the approach is easy to understand, and provides new insights as a useful complement to existing mostly static methods. The approach is universal, understandable, and applicable to a wide variety of fields at both the macro and micro levels. Since time distance view provides an additional dimension of temporal disparity, results by other methods are left unchanged but new conclusions can be reached.

Gender inequality in life expectancy – static distance and time distance

In Figure 1 we take the example of gender disparities in life expectancy at birth for EU27 aggregates. One way is to compare time series at a given point in time, i.e. in our case the static gap in life expectancy between women and men in 2010. The absolute difference amounted to 5.9 years; the index was 107.7.

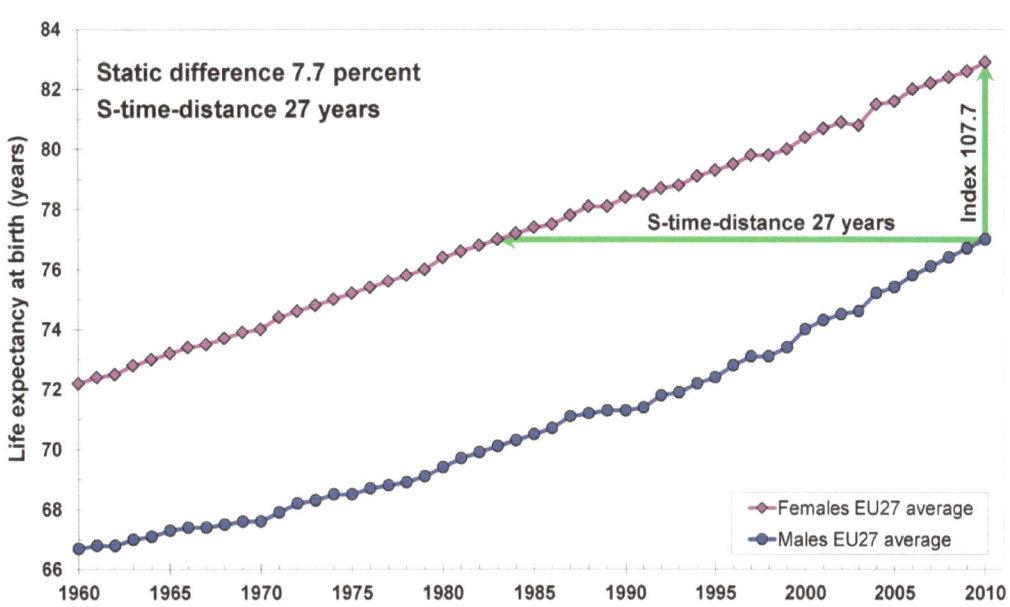

FIGURE 1 Gender disparities in life expectancy at birth, EU27 average in 2010: static index and time distance
SOURCE: Own calculations based on Eurostat (2006, 2013).

Another dimension of the degree of disparity is taking into consideration the distance in years when men and women reached the same reference level of the variable, in our case the life expectancy for men in 2010 was reached by women already in 1983 (i.e. 27 years earlier): S-time-distance amounted to 27 years.

The figure illustrates these two dimensions of gender disparities in life expectancy and indicates that perceptions of the size of this gap can be very different depending on the statistical measure used. Here the static difference between two lines in 2010 is less than 8 percent (which may appear to be small) while the time distance is 27 years (which gives a very different perception of the magnitude of the gap). The perception of wellbeing and of the degree of disparity is subjective. For realistic evaluation of the situation we need both measures. Sicherl (2011a) discusses the concept of 'overall degree of disparity' defined as proximity in the indicator space as well as in time, which has the potential to bring new additional understanding for numerous issues in economics, management, research, and statistics. Further discussion on inter-temporal aspect of wellbeing will be available in Sicherl (in press). Different people will give different subjective weights to the static and time distance dimension of disparity and they might be also very different for different indicators.

A brief definition of two novel statistical measures: S-time-distance and S-time-step

The statistical measure **S-time-distance** measures the distance (proximity) in time between the points in time when the two series compared reach a specified level of the indicator X. For instance, the HDI level of 0.55 was attained in China in 1996, in India in 2011, S-time-distance amounts to 15 years (2011 minus 1996). This means that India was lagging in time for 15 years or that China was leading by 15 years. **S-time-distance** for a given level of X_L is defined as:

$$S_{ij} (X_L) = \Delta t (X_L) = t_i (X_L) - t_j (X_L) \qquad (1)$$

The **S-time-step** measures the time elapsed between two levels of a time-series, providing an alternative description of its growth rate, measuring the growth of a series by using the inverse relation to the conventional $\Delta X/\Delta t$ growth rate metrics. For instance, the very high human development group needed in the past about 5.5 years to increase the life expectancy from 79 years to 80 years; this is a complementary description of the dynamics of life expectancy to the conventional growth rate matrix, which would described the dynamics as about 0.2 percentage per year. Both measures are valid description of the dynamics of change, while for general public S-time-step might be even easier to understand. **S-time-step** is expressed in units of time and is defined as:

$$S_i (\Delta X_L) = [t_i (X_L + \Delta X) - t_i (X_L)]/\Delta X \qquad (2)$$

Further information on the time distance methodology and applications are available in numerous earlier publications like Kyklos (Sicherl, 1973), IB Revija (Sicherl, 1999), Social Indicators Research (Sicherl, 2007), in the paper published by OECD Statistics Directorate (Sicherl, 2011a), and most extensively in the book 'Time Distance in Economics and Statistics' (Sicherl, 2012). More information is available in Appendix A1.

World inequalities in life expectancy at birth

We shall use the indicator life expectancy at birth in this predominant methodological chapter for two reasons. Firstly, life expectancy is a very important indicator of wellbeing and via direct transformation into health index one of the three HDI component indices. Secondly, the discussion in terms of life expectancy provides very understandable new information of the time distance perspective in this indicator without being influenced by the assumptions of the transformation procedures in calculating other indices.

Time distance is an innovative approach for looking at time-series data providing a broader dynamic analytical framework, complementing rather than replacing the existing mostly static measures. It is a generic approach, expressed in time units, easy to understand, especially in the applications in this report for life expectancy and HDI. In Figure 2 the rows are defined by the levels of life expectancy at birth from 40 years to 82 years, the units of comparison are 13 countries, a selection of countries from all four human development groups for the period 1980-2012, and the long-term trend for Sweden as the comparator. The years shown in the table are the approximate time when such levels of life expectancy were attained in the selected countries.

Time matrix is an original possibility of additional presentation of time series data. In the usual time series table data of the indicator (e.g. life expectancy) are organised in relation to the descriptors, like units (e.g. countries) and time (e.g. years). The time matrix presents the original data (or some approximations) in an alternative way: descriptors are units and levels of the indicator and the value in the field of the table are times when such levels were attained. Calculating these times by interpolations may pose a small problem of the degree of accuracy compared to the original data, but it offers additional understanding about the time dimension of disparities and a good summary overview.

There are several methods of calculating time distances and comparing them also with static measures, for three types of comparisons: the level of the indicators, their dynamics, and comparisons of levels relative to a benchmark (see Sicherl, 2011a). The first comparison can start with time matrix visualisation of the selected indicator over many units and over time (Figure 2).

In the time matrix data are arranged by selected levels of indicators showing in which year these levels of the indicators were achieved by given country. This format of level-time matrix is easily understood by everybody, at the same time it provides also a simple visualisation tool for many units over time. The observed level-time table-graph in yellow colour shows the range of values achieved for a given country over the period from available data.

HDI Rank	1	2	45	51	90	94	101	121	136	145	146	146	186	8
LEXP Level	Norway	Australia	Argentina	Uruguay	Turkey	Tunisia	China	Indonesia	India	Kenya	Pakistan	Bangladesh	Niger	Sweden
82		2012												
81	2011	2005												2008
80	2006	2002												2002
79	2001	1998												1997
78	1997	1994												1992
77	1992	1991		2011										1987
76	1984	1987	2012	2006										1981
75		1983	2006	2001										1975
74			2001	1997	2011	2008								1965
73			1997	1992	2008	2002	2009							1958
72			1992	1988	2005	1999	2004							1953
71			1988	1983	2003	1996	1999							1950
70			1983		2001	1994	1993							1947
69					1999	1991	1988	2010				2011		1946
68					1998	1989	1984	2008				2008		1944
67					1996	1988	1980	2005				2005		1941
66					1995	1986		2001				2003		1939
65					1993	1984		1998	2010		2009	2001		1937
64					1991	1983		1995	2007		2005	1999		1932
63					1990	1981		1993	2004		2000	1997		1931
62					1988			1990	2001		1995	1995		1928
61					1987			1988	1998		1991	1993		1921
60					1985			1985	1995		1988	1991		1921
59					1984			1983	1992	1990	1984	1989		1920
58					1982			1981	1989	1992	1980	1987		1920
57					1981				1986	2011		1984		1919
56									1982	2009		1982		1906
55										2008			2012	1905
54										2006			2009	1902
53										2004			2007	1901
52													2006	1900
51													2004	1899
50													2003	1886
49													2001	1885
48													2000	1880
47													1998	1878
46													1997	1877
45													1995	1876
44													1994	1870
43													1992	1870
42													1991	1869
41													1988	1869
40													1983	1858

FIGURE 2 Time matrix for life expectancy at birth for selected countries and for benchmark Sweden

SOURCE: Own calculations based on data from UNDP (2013b), for Sweden before 1980 Mitchell (2003).

This allows for a quick level comparison:

- of the situation across the selected countries
- of how many steps over levels of indicators a given country has progressed, which is an additional indication of the dynamics in the country.

There is a wealth of information and of possible comparisons in the Figure 2 that cannot be discussed here in detail. At the glance one can visually observe that there are substantial differences in life expectancy between the analysed countries. On the other hand, as countries are ordered by the rank of the overall human development index it is clear that positions of some countries with respect to life expectancy are different than that in HDI.

The UNDP database (UNDP, 2013b) covers the time series for HDI indices for the period from 1980 to 2012. The same period was taken for life expectancy in the time matrix in Figure 2 and that period can be compared to the history of Sweden.

Comparing horizontally, in this period life expectancy for Sweden, Norway, and Australia was in the range from 76 to 81 years, for Australia a year more in both directions. On the other hand, the range in Niger was from 40 to 55 years of life expectancy, a large increase in absolute terms but still much below more developed countries. Values for life expectancy are for these countries ordered in similar way as the numbers of the HDI ranks. However, at a glance it can be seen that Pakistan and especially Bangladesh are better positioned for life expectancy than for the overall HDI rank. Comparing vertically in the time matrix the dynamics of progress of life expectancy can be visually noticed. Turkey, Niger, and Bangladesh showed the greatest number of upward steps, with increases of about 18, 16, and 14 years of life expectancy over the period. S-time-step as a measure of speed will be shown in Figure 4.

Apart from the visualisation of levels over the analysed period from the level-time matrix in Figure 2 we can derive two statistical measures, expressed in standardized units of time: S-time-distance and S-time-step. S-time-distances in Figure 3 for selected levels of life expectancy are arrived at by subtracting the respective times for a given unit and the times for the benchmark unit (long trend for Sweden) in the level-time matrix in Figure 2. On the other hand, we get S-time-step (in years) by subtracting the respective times for consecutive levels of the variable for each unit by columns in the time matrix in Figure 2. As mentioned earlier, this is a possible measure of the dynamic characteristics of a series. There are other possibilities for these calculations from the original data. However, the estimation from the time matrix is very simple to understand the relationships of the new insights provided by the two novel statistical measures.

The estimates of time lead or time lag from the selected benchmark in Figure 3 show that at national levels the world inequalities in life expectancy are very high. Even more, if one would use only data from the 1980-2012 period from the UNDP database (UNDP, 2013b) the highest value of the time lag that can be determined from this data would amount to 32 years (length of the period of available data). From the selected countries in the time matrix in Figure 2 the time lag behind leaders Australia and Norway can be calculated only for Argentina and Uruguay. Namely, the next countries Turkey and Tunisia reached the level of life expectancy of only 74 years, which is less than values of Australia and Norway in the beginning of 1980's.

HDI Rank / LEXP Level	1 Norway	2 Australia	45 Argentina	51 Uruguay	90 Turkey	94 Tunisia	101 China	121 Indonesia	136 India	145 Kenya	146 Pakistan	146 Bangladesh	186 Niger	8 Sweden
82														
81	3	-3												0
80	3	0												0
79	4	1												0
78	5	2												0
77	6	4		24										0
76	3	6	30	25										0
75		8	31	26										0
74			36	31	46	43								0
73			39	34	50	44	51							0
72			39	35	52	45	51							0
71			38	34	53	46	49							0
70			35		54	46	46							0
69					54	45	43	65				66		0
68					53	45	40	63				64		0
67					55	47	39	64				64		0
66					56	47		63				64		0
65					56	47		61	72		72	63		0
64					59	51		63	75		72	67		0
63					59	50		61	73		68	65		0
62					61			62	74		68	67		0
61					66			67	77		70	72		0
60					65			65	75		67	70		0
59					64			63	72	70	64	69		0
58					63			61	69	72	61	67		0
57					62				66	92		65		0
56									77	103		76		0
55										103			107	0
54										105			108	0
53										103			106	0
52													106	0
51													105	0
50													117	0
49													116	0
48													119	0
47													120	0
46													120	0
45													119	0
44													124	0
43													123	0
42													121	0
41													118	0
40													125	0

FIGURE 3 S-time-distances (in years) indicating lag or lead behind the benchmark of long-term trend for Sweden

SOURCE: Own calculation based on data in Figure 2.

Only when we have introduced as benchmark long-term trends for Sweden we were able to indicate the perception of the magnitude of inequalities in the time distance dimension. For 2012 level of life expectancy in Niger one has to go back in the history of Sweden to find that level in year 1905, indicating the S-time-distance of about 107 years.

Time distances in Figure 3 are arranged by the levels of the indicator as in the time matrix in Figure 2. For the recent levels of life expectancy (top positions in the columns in Figure 3) the degree of disparity in time behind benchmark Sweden is very high, for Uruguay and Argentina about 24 and 30 years, for Turkey and Tunisia about 43 and 46 years, 51 years for China, around 65 for Indonesia and Bangladesh, between 70 and 72 years for Kenya, Pakistan, and India, for Niger more than 100 years. This is a new way to assess the reality by applying the novel statistical methodology.

Different perception of inequality based on percentage and time distance measures

We have used life expectancy as the indicator to demonstrate that there are different possible statistical measures that can be used to describe the magnitude of inequalities. Below we are showing the comparison of the results for inequality in life expectancy using three descriptive statistical measures: absolute difference, percentage difference, and S-time-distance.

Comparison	Absolute difference	Percantage difference	S-time-distance (years)
Sweden - China	7.9	9.7%	51
Sweden - Lithuania	9.1	11.2%	55
Sweden - Niger	26.5	32.5%	107
VHHD - HHD	6.7	8.4%	32
HHD - MHD	3.5	4.8%	12
MHD - LHD	10.8	15.5%	> 32

TABLE 1 The perception of the magnitude of the differences in life expectancy may differ depending on the measure used
SOURCE: Own calculations based on data from UNDP (2013b), for Sweden before 1980 Mitchell (2003).

Similar to the example in Figure 1 the cases in this table indicate that perceptions of the size of this gap can be very different depending on the statistical measure used. The static difference against Sweden was less than 10 percent for China and 11 percent for Lithuania (which may appear to be small) while the S-time-distance was 51 and 55 years, respectively (which gives a very different perception of the magnitude of the gap). The earlier comments showed how the time distance for the case for Niger behind Sweden was beyond 100 years, i.e. about twice of the above two countries.

The next three examples refer to the differences in averages of life expectancy between the four human development groups as defined in the HDI Report: very high (VHHD), high (HHD), medium (MHD), and low (LHD) group. Life expectancy in the very high group is higher than in the high group for 6.7 years; in percentage terms the high group is 8.4 percent lower (which in comparisons with inequality in other indicators like income would be perceived as small). Time delay was 32 years as life expectancy for high group in 2012 was at the level of very high group in 1980, indicating a very large and persisting degree of inequality. The disparity between high and medium group is smaller, about 5 percent and 12 years. So the medium group is closing up faster to the high group than the low group to the medium group; the percentage difference is 15.5 percent, while the S-time-distance is more than 32 years as there in no intersection over the three decades of the analysed period.

Last but not least: S-time-step as an additional measure of dynamics

LEXP Level	Human development group			
	Very high	High	Medium	Low
80	5.5			
79	4.3			
78	4.4			
77	4.5			
76	4.7			
75	4.8			
74				
73		3.5		
72		3.3		
71		3.3		
70		4.6		
69		4.8	3.7	
68		3.6	4.5	
67		3.3	4.2	
66		3.3	4.2	
65			3.7	
64			3.2	
63			3.2	
62				
61				
60				
59				2.5
58				2.5
57				2.3
56				2.6
55				3.4
54				5.3
53				4.9
52				4.3
51				

FIGURE 4 S-time-step (in years) as an additional measure of dynamics of life expectancy
How many years were needed to reach the next level of the indicator
SOURCE: Own calculations based on data from UNDP (2013b).

As explained earlier in addition to the S-time-distance measure there is also a novel statistical measure S-time-step measuring the time elapsed between two selected levels of a time series. In Figure 4 this additional measure of dynamics is shown for life expectancy, i.e. how many years were needed to reach the next level of the life expectancy. In this figure the S-time-step (in years) is shown for the life expectancy of the four human development groups. In this case the very high group needed in the past about 5.5 years to increase the life expectancy from 79 years to 80 years; the low group needed 2.5 years to increase the life expectancy from 58 years to 59 years.

The S-time-step measure is very easy to understand, for 1 year of increase of life expectancy at the very high level about 5.5 years were needed, for the low group about 2.5 years were needed for 1 year of increase in life expectancy at much lower level. This is a complementary description of the dynamics of life expectancy to the conventional growth rate matrix, which would described the dynamics as about 0.2 percentage per year for the very high group and about 0.7 percentage per year for the low group for the discussed increase in the life expectancy levels. Both measures are valid description of the dynamics of change. For general public it might be even easier to understand that in the current past for one year of increase in life expectancy about 5.5 years in the very high group and 2.5 years for the low group were needed.

Methodological conclusions and results for health index

It was shown how two additional descriptive statistical measures S-time-distance and S-time-step can usefully complement the conventional mostly static framework. As indicated earlier we used the indicator life expectancy at birth in this predominant methodological chapter for two reasons. Table 1 has shown that the perception of the magnitude of the differences in life expectancy may differ depending on the measure used; static inequalities seemed to give smaller and time distances larger perceptions of the degree of inequality. Besides the fact that the analysis provided new insights of the world situation in inequalities in life expectancy in the dynamic framework these examples also indicate the methodology that will be used in analysing world disparities in other human development indicators.

As in the UNDP analysis health index is based on the transformation of the differences in levels of life expectancy in the index format it means that the time distances calculated for absolute levels of life expectancy will stay the same for the health index between respective units, as it is the methodological characteristics of S-time-distance measure that linear transformations of time series will leave S-time-distances unchanged.

When considering time distances that include both past realisations and future projections, it is important to distinguish between backward looking (ex post) and forward looking (ex ante) S-time-distances; while the first type of measure belongs to the domain of descriptive statistics based on known facts, the second type may allow describing the results of alternative policies in the future. While the time distance approach is not a forecasting tool, it provides a very useful innovative presentation of complex data sets.

We have shown that one way of calculating S-time-distance and S-time-step measures is to use the earlier shown time matrix format. However, even by itself level-time matrix can be used in publications, web pages, and other software as one of the easily understandable first level summary visualisation to help 'Turning Statistics into Knowledge' (Sicherl, 2011a). For example it was used for 'Visualization of 50 years of OECD countries at a glance' (Sicherl, 2011b).

Chapter 3

TRENDS IN WORLD INEQUALITIES IN HUMAN DEVELOPMENT INDEX

The Human Development Index (HDI) is a composite indicator with well documented database covering over three decades of trends 1980-2012 (UNDP, 2013a). Over this period some variables were revised taking into account measurement improvements and the wide array of conceptually solid measures, including additional disaggregations. HDI combines health index, education index, and income index and is a partial measure that attempts to provide a broad vision of the advance of countries in furthering capabilities (Klugman et al., 2011).

Much effort has been invested at building statistical database on national and international levels, as in a notionally related field of Millennium Development Goals (MDG). Measurement is costly and it is important to exploit existing data efficiently for building knowledge and for policy debate. Describing and perceiving inequalities in terms of percentages and ranks is not enough. Development processes take place in time and to get additional insights from existing data we complement the static measures of inequality by measuring the gap in time when two compared countries achieved the same level of HDI (e.g., the HDI level of 0.55 was attained in China in 1996, in India in 2011, the latter lagging in time 15 years). Figure 5 provides quick visual overview over trends of the four human development (HD) groups for the period 1980-2012 calculated on the basis of the UNDP (2013b) data.

The developments in the 1980-2012 period for Human Development Index (HDI), non-income HDI, and income index for the four HD groups are presented in the time matrix format, which shows the time when a given indicator level was attained. The year presented in bold show the latest available year for a given selected level of the indicator. It can help to quickly observe whether there was a noticeable decrease in later years in the observed period.

Trends over the three decades for four human development groups in HDI, non-income HDI, and income index

The range of values over the three decades for the four HD groups was 0.31 - 0.92. There were substantial improvements in all indices, but disparities in the world remain very large.

Level	HDI Human Development				Non-income HDI Human Development				Income index Human Development			
	Very high	High	Medium	Low	Very high	High	Medium	Low	Very high	High	Medium	Low
0.92					2009							
0.91					2006							
0.90	2010				2004							
0.89	2005				2002							
0.88	2003				2000							
0.87	2001				1999							
0.86	1999				1997							
0.85	1997				1995				2004			
0.84	1995				1994				2000			
0.83	1993				1992				1997			
0.82	1991				1990				1993			
0.81	1988				1989				1989			
0.80	1986				1987				1986			
0.79	1984				1985				1984			
0.78	1982				1983	2012			1981			
0.77					1981	2009						
0.76						2007						
0.75		2010				2006						
0.74		2007				2004						
0.73		2006				2003						
0.72		2004				2002						
0.71		2003				2000						
0.70		2001				1999				2012		
0.69		1999				1997				2010		
0.68		1996				1996				2006		
0.67		1994				1994				2004		
0.66		1991				1993	2012			2003		
0.65		1989				1991	2009			2001		
0.64		1987	2012			1990	2007					
0.63		1985	2010			1988	2006					
0.62		1983	2008			1987	2005					
0.61		1981	2007			1986	2003					
0.60			2006			1984	2002					
0.59			2005			1983	2001				2012	
0.58			2004			1982	1999				2011	
0.57			2003			1980	1998				2010	
0.56			2001				1996				2009	
0.55			2000				1994				2008	
0.54			1999				1993				2007	
0.53			1997				1991				2006	
0.52			1996				1989				2005	
0.51			1994				1988				2004	
0.50			1993				1986				2003	
0.49			1991				1985				2002	
0.48			1990				1983	2010			2001	
0.47			1988				1982	2008			2000	
0.46			1987	2010			1980	2007			1998	
0.45			1985	2008				2006			1997	
0.44			1983	2007				2005			1996	
0.43			1982	2006				2004			1994	
0.42			1980	2004				2003			1993	
0.41				2003				2001			1991	2011
0.40				2002				2000			1990	2009
0.39				2001				1998			1988	2007
0.38				1999				1996			1986	2005
0.37				1996				1993			1985	2004
0.36				1993				1991			1983	2002
0.35				1990				1988			1981	1997
0.34				1987				1987				
0.33				1984				1985				
0.32				1981				1983				
0.31								1981				

Notes in figure:

> Very high group is leading the high group by more than 32 years.

> For non-income HDI the time distances between the HD groups are rounded 29 years, 19 years, and 27 years.

> The largest gaps and largest time distances are in income index.

> Medium group is falling behind the high group for 25 years.

> Low group is lagging medium group for 23 years.

FIGURE 5 A quick visual overview over the four HD groups (trends 1980-2012)
SOURCE: Own calculations based on data from UNDP (2013b).

It can be seen at a glance the largest gaps and largest time distances were in income index, which means that the world disparities in the non-income HDI are considerably smaller than in the overall Human Development Index. Describing the inequalities for HDI between the four HD groups it is shown that very high group is leading the high group by more than 32 years, medium group is falling behind the high group for 25 years, and low group is lagging medium group for 23 years.

For non-income HDI the time distances between the HD groups are rounded 29 years, 19 years, and 27 years; i.e. in the order of magnitude of about 74 years between first and last group. The time gaps are very large between very high and high group, as well as between high and medium groups for income index, as in both cases they need to be at least more than 32 years (as in the available data over the 32 years of the analysed period 1980-2012 the respective groups have never reached the same level of the income index). This means that the time gap must have been considerably higher than 32 years (if longer time series of the index would allow us to calculate the times when the same level of the income index were attained in the past).

Looking at the Figure 5 S-time-distance values can give a rough impression of the magnitude of world inequality expressed as gap in time. A very approximate indication of the time distance between the very high and the low group could be about 74 years for non-income HDI, about 82 years for HDI, and about 100 years for income index. While these values need to be approximations because of short time series of available data, the time distance estimates are relevant statistical descriptive measures of the situation easily understandable by everyone, balancing the static view.

Trends and S-time-distance for HDI for 13 selected countries over the range of all 187 countries

Figure 6 gives a quick visual overview of HDI over selected countries (trends 1980-2012). In each of the four human development groups we selected some countries to make a provisional assessment over the range of all 187 countries. The range of HDI values over the three decades is 0.18 - 0.95. Again, there were substantial improvements in these selected countries in HDI in the analysed period but disparities remain, as expected, even larger as between the four groups, which amounted to about 82 years. In the low group about 40 countries had value HDI below 0.50, while the average for the very high group was 0.90. To indicate the magnitude of the time lag between the lowest and the highest countries we can additionally use life expectancy (Sicherl, 2012), e.g. about three quarters of the low HD group were lagging benchmark Sweden between 90 and 130 years.

Group	Very high			High			Medium			Low			
HDI Rank	1	2	45	51	90	94	101	121	136	145	146	146	186
Country	Norway	Australia	Argentina	Uruguay	Turkey	Tunisia	China	Indonesia	India	Kenya	Pakistan	Bangladesh	Niger
0.95	**2009**												
0.94	2003												
0.93	2002	**2007**											
0.92	2000	2002											
0.91	1998	1999											
0.90	1997	1996											
0.89	1995	1993											
0.88	1994	1990											
0.87	1993	1986											
0.86	1991	1981											
0.85	1990												
0.84	1988												
0.83	1985												
0.82	1983												
0.81	1981		**2011**										
0.80			2009										
0.79			2007	**2011**									
0.78			2006	2009									
0.77			2005	2007									
0.76			2002	2006									
0.75			1999	2005									
0.74			1997	2000									
0.73			1995	1998									
0.72			1994	1996	**2011**								
0.71			1992	1994	2009	**2011**							
0.70			1990	1991	2007	2008							
0.69			1986	1989	2006	2006	**2010**						
0.68			1982	1986	2004	2005	2009						
0.67				1982	2003	2004	2008						
0.66					2002	2002	2007						
0.65					2001	2001	2006						
0.64					1999	2000	2005						
0.63					1998	1999	2004						
0.62					1997	1998	2003	**2010**					
0.61					1995	1996	2002	2009					
0.60					1994	1995	2001	2008					
0.59					1993	1994	2000	2007					
0.58					1991	1993	1999	2006					
0.57					1990	1992	1998	2004					
0.56					1989	1991	1997	2003					
0.55					1988	1990	1996	2001	**2011**				
0.54					1987	1989	1995	2000	2009				
0.53					1986	1988	1994	1998	2008				
0.52					1985	1986	1993	1997	2007				
0.51					1984	1985	1992	1995	2005	**2010**	**2010**	**2011**	
0.50					1983	1984	1991	1993	2004	2009	2008	2009	
0.49					1982	1983	1989	1992	2003	2007	2006	2007	
0.48					1981	1982	1988	1990	2002	2006	2005	2006	
0.47						1981	1987	1988	2001	2005	2004	2005	
0.46						1980	1986	1987	1999	2003	2003	2003	
0.45							1985	1985	1998	2001	2002	2002	
0.44							1984	1983	1996	1984	2002	2001	
0.43							1983	1981	1994	1982	2001	2000	
0.42							1981		1992		2000	1998	
0.41							1980		1990		1998	1997	
0.40									1988		1995	1995	
0.39									1987		1992	1994	
0.38									1985		1989	1993	
0.37									1984		1987	1991	
0.36									1982		1985	1990	
0.35									1981		1983	1988	
0.34											1981	1986	
0.33												1984	
0.32												1982	
0.31													
0.30													**2011**
0.29													2009
0.28													2007
0.27													2005
0.26													2004
0.25													2002
0.24													2001
0.23													1999
0.22													1996
0.21													1993
0.20													1991
0.19													1986
0.18													1981

FIGURE 6 A quick visual overview of HDI over selected countries (trends 1980-2012)
SOURCE: Own calculations based on data from Human Development Report 2013, UNDP (2013a).

Figure 7 calculates the respective S-time-distances (from the time matrix in Figure 6), by using China (which was one the best performers) as an interesting benchmark to which other countries are compared.

Group	Very high			High			Medium			Low			
HDI Rank	1	2	45	51	90	94	101	121	136	145	146	146	186
Country	Norway	Australia	Argentina	Uruguay	Turkey	Tunisia	China	Indonesia	India	Kenya	Pakistan	Bangladesh	Niger
0.69			-24	-21	-5	-4	0						
0.68			-27	-23	-5	-4	0						
0.67				-26	-5	-4	0						
0.66					-5	-4	0						
0.65					-5	-5	0						
0.64					-6	-5	0						
0.63					-6	-6	0						
0.62					-6	-6	0	7					
0.61					-7	-6	0	7					
0.60					-7	-6	0	7					
0.59					-7	-6	0	7					
0.58					-8	-6	0	7					
0.57					-8	-6	0	6					
0.56					-8	-6	0	6					
0.55					-8	-6	0	6	15				
0.54					-8	-6	0	5	14				
0.53					-8	-6	0	5	14				
0.52					-8	-6	0	4	14				
0.51					-8	-6	0	4	14	18	18	19	
0.50					-8	-6	0	3	14	18	17	18	
0.49					-8	-6	0	2	14	17	17	18	
0.48					-8	-6	0	2	14	18	16	18	
0.47						-6	0	1	14	17	17	18	
0.46						-6	0	1	13	17	17	17	
0.45							0	0	13	16	17	17	
0.44							0	-1	12	0	18	17	
0.43							0	-1	11	-1	18	17	
0.42							0		10		19	17	
0.41							0		10		17	16	

S-time-distance (years):   (-) time lead,   (+) time lag   from benchmark China

Text box (left): China was close to the lowest countries in the high human development group behind Turkey for 5 years, and for about 24 years behind one of the lowest countries in the very high human development group Argentina.

Text box (right): China was ahead of Bangladesh for 19 years, for Pakistan 18 years, and for India 15 years.

FIGURE 7 S-time-distance in years as a time measure of the gap: (-) time lead, (+) time lag from benchmark China for a given level of HDI
SOURCE: Own calculations based on data in Figure 6.

China was close to the lowest countries in the high human development group (behind Turkey for 5 years) and is still nearly 24 years behind Argentina at the lower end of the very high human development group; in turn Argentina is about 30 years behind the leading countries like Norway and Australia. About 15 countries of the low group have still not reached the level of China in 1980. China was ahead of Bangladesh for 19 years, for Pakistan 18 years, and for India 15 years.

Chapter 4

OVERALL HUMAN DEVELOPMENT INDEX, HEALTH, EDUCATION, AND INCOME COMPONENTS

In this chapter the earlier analysis for the HDI and non-income HDI as well as analysis of inequalities between selected countries from the four HD groups from Norway to Niger will be extended to the analysis of the three main HDI components – health, education, and income index over the analysed period 1980-2012.

The time matrix in the Figure 8 shows the world view over 4 HD groups and 4 indices. In the time matrix one can compare in two directions: comparing between the four groups - very high (VHHD), high (HHD), medium (MHD), and low (LHD) group - for a given index and/or comparing the four indices within the given HD group. In Figure 8 data are arranged for the first direction of comparison, but the second direction can be seen by rearranging the same data.

Comparisons of world inequalities over four HD groups and four indices (trends 1980-2012)

In general health index is the highest component attained, followed by education and income (for MHD in LHD income is higher than education). While for HDI there is a break of more than 32 years between the very high and high HD group, in the health index such a break is between medium and low HD group, while for income index such large gaps appeared between very high and high group as well as between high and medium group. For education index the trends were such that levels achieved over the period by the two consecutive compared groups allowed the calculation of the approximate S-time-distance between the groups.

Looking at time distances between the HD groups there are interesting differences for the four indices. For the overall HDI the time distances between the HD groups are more than 32 years, 25 years, and 23 years. The smallest time distances for the components are those for education index. For education index the time distances between the HD groups are 26 years, 21 years, and 22 years. For health index the time distances between the HD groups are more than 32 years, 12 years, and more than 32 years. For income index the respective time distances between the HD groups are the largest, showing the large gaps in income levels and large time distances.

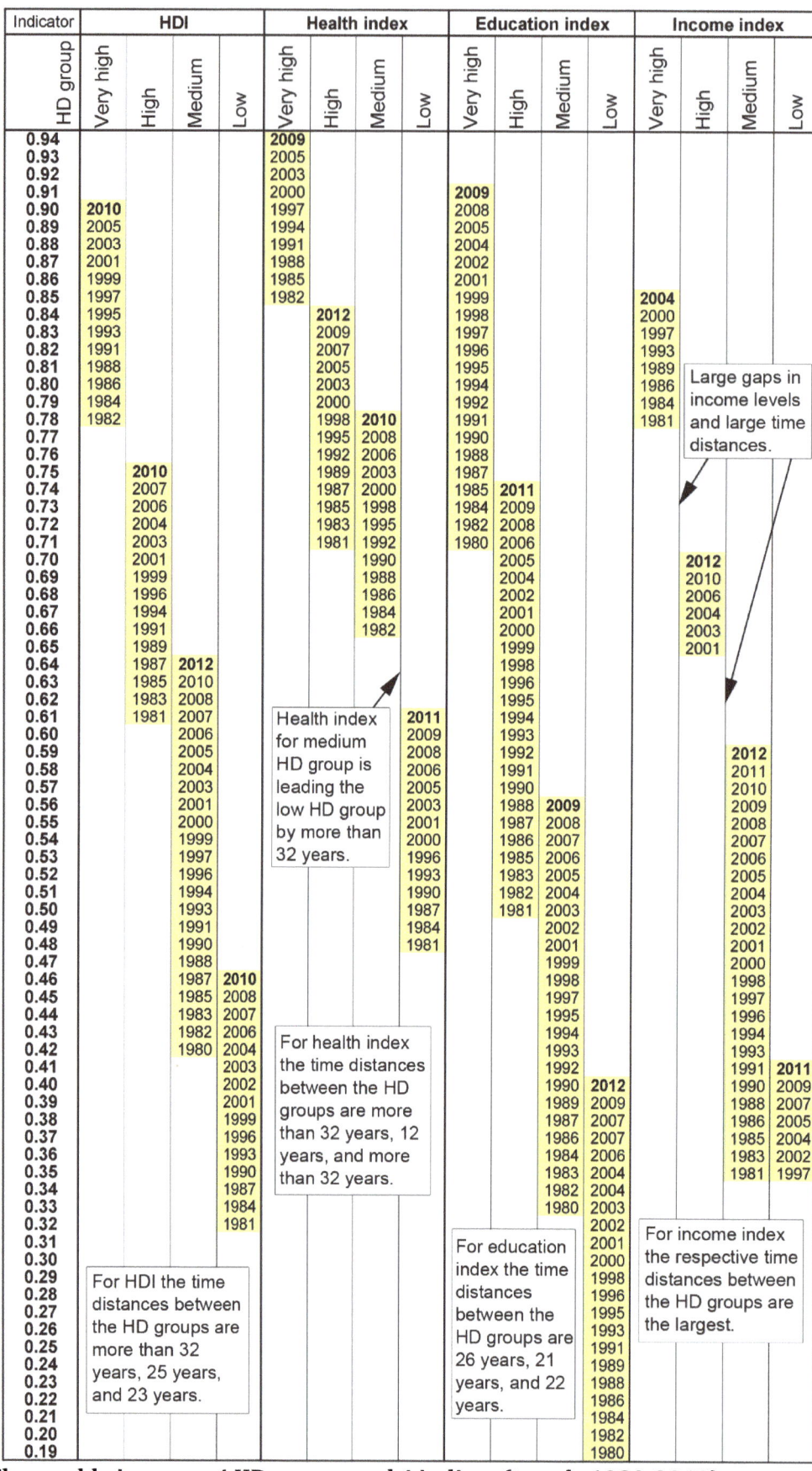

FIGURE 8 The world view over 4 HD groups and 4 indices (trends 1980-2012)
SOURCE: Own calculations based on data from UNDP (2013b).

By comparing the three component indices within each HD groups it is shown that the time distances between the levels of the three indices for averages for very high group (VHHD) are much smaller than for other groups. The level of health index is the highest, the level of education index is lagging behind the level of health index for 9 years (level 0.91 was achieved in 2000 and 2009) and that of income index at the lower level for 22 years (the same level of index 0.85 was achieved in 1982, 1999, and 2004, respectively). The time lag of income index behind education is low (5 years).

For the high HD group education index is lagging behind health index for 24 years and income index is lagging for more than 32 years; the lag of income index behind education is low. For the medium HD group and low HD group the value of health index is for both groups is so high that it is more than 32 years ahead of the levels for the income and education index. As mentioned before, for the medium HD group and low HD group the value of the income index was higher than that of education index, which is different order than for the very high and high HD groups.

S-time-step as a measure of dynamics over all human development groups

Figure 9 presents the values of S-time-step showing how many years were needed to reach the next level of indicator in the past. This quick visual overview over all human development groups (trends 1980-2012) for the four indices gives the additional statistical measure of dynamics for these indices in easily understandable time units.

Across the three component indices the fastest dynamics is shown for the education index where the S-time-step indicates that on the average about 1.4 years were in the past needed for the increase of one level of the education index (0.01). The dynamics of the health index was slower as it was needed between 2.3 and 3 years for one unit of increase on the average over the period. While the level of health index was the highest of all components in all HD groups the dynamics is slower, it takes more time for a unit increase than education index in all four HD groups. S-time-step was higher also than that for the income index in the very high group and very much so in the medium HD group where the very high dynamics in the income index was influenced by the income growth in China. Namely, the time needed to increase one unit of the income index varies from 1.3 years for medium, to 2.4 years for low and 3.4 years for very high HD group. While past performance should not be simply extrapolated into the future, S-time-step can provide a hint how fast higher levels of indices could be achieved in a more simple understandable terms than dynamics expressed in percentage terms which very much depends on the starting levels; they are for these indices very different between HD groups and even more between individual countries.

HD group	Very high				High				Medium				Low			
Index	HDI	Health	Education	Income	HDI	Health	Education	Income	HDI	Health	Education	Income	HDI	Health	Education	Income
0.94		3.3														
0.93		2.7														
0.92		2.6														
0.91		2.9	1.8													
0.90	4.2	2.9	2.5													
0.89	2.4	2.9	1.4													
0.88	2.3	3.0	1.4													
0.87	2.1	3.0	1.4													
0.86	2.0	3.0	1.3													
0.85	2.0		1.2	3.8												
0.84	2.0		1.2	3.7		2.5										
0.83	2.0		1.2	3.7		2.0										
0.82	2.2		1.2	3.6		2.2										
0.81	2.3		1.2	2.9		2.2										
0.80	2.3		1.2	2.9		2.2										
0.79	2.3		1.2	2.9		2.8										
0.78			1.2			2.9				2.4						
0.77			1.6			2.9				2.3						
0.76			1.6			2.6				2.7						
0.75			1.6		2.2	2.1				2.8						
0.74			1.6		1.6	2.1	2.4			2.7						
0.73			1.6		1.5	2.1	1.1			2.7						
0.72			1.6		1.7	2.1	1.5			2.7						
0.71					1.7		1.1			2.6						
0.70					2.1		1.3	2.5		2.0						
0.69					2.6		1.3	3.5		2.0						
0.68					2.6		1.3	1.6		2.0						
0.67					2.6		1.2	1.9		2.0						
0.66					2.2		1.2	1.9								
0.65					2.0		1.2									
0.64					2.0		1.1		2.1							
0.63					2.0		1.2		1.4							
0.62					2.0		1.1		1.3							
0.61							1.2		1.0						1.7	
0.60							1.2		1.0						1.6	
0.59							1.1		1.2			1.2			1.4	
0.58							1.2		1.3			1.0			1.6	
0.57							1.2		1.3			1.0			1.6	
0.56							1.2		1.3		1.3	1.1			1.6	
0.55							1.2		1.4		1.0	1.0			1.8	
0.54							1.2		1.5		1.0	0.7			3.3	
0.53							1.2		1.5		1.1	0.8			3.3	
0.52							1.2		1.5		1.0	1.0			3.3	
0.51							1.2		1.5		1.0	1.1			2.8	
0.50									1.5		1.0	1.1			2.8	
0.49									1.5		1.0	1.1			2.8	
0.48									1.6		1.2	1.2				
0.47									1.6		1.3	1.4				
0.46									1.6		1.3	1.4	1.5			
0.45									1.6		1.3	1.4	1.5			
0.44									1.6		1.3	1.4	1.0			
0.43									1.6		1.3	1.4	1.3			
0.42											1.3	1.4	1.3			
0.41											1.3	1.3	1.3			2.5
0.40										1.4	1.8	1.3			3.5	2.1
0.39										1.4	1.8	2.1			1.1	1.3
0.38										1.5	1.8	2.9			0.9	1.7
0.37										1.5	1.8	2.9			0.9	2.1
0.36										1.5	1.8	2.9			1.1	5.0
0.35										1.5		2.9			0.9	
0.34										1.4		2.9			0.9	
0.33												2.9			0.9	
0.32															0.9	
0.31															0.9	
0.30															1.8	
0.29															1.8	
0.28															1.8	
0.27															1.8	
0.26															1.8	
0.25															1.8	
0.24															1.9	
0.23															1.8	
0.22															1.8	
0.21															1.9	
0.20															1.8	
0.19																

Education index shows the highest dynamics: S-time-step is about 1.4 years in all HD groups.

The time needed to increase one unit of the income index varies from 1.3 years for medium, to 2.4 years for low and 3.4 years for very high HD group.

S-time-step for health index varies between 2.3 and 3 years.

FIGURE 9 S-time-step: how many years were needed to reach the next level of the indicator
A quick visual overview of dynamics over all HD groups (trends 1980-2012)
SOURCE: Own calculations based on data from UNDP (2013b).

Chapter 5

AN OVERVIEW OVER 187 COUNTRIES

TIME DISTANCE INEQUALITIES WITHIN THE FOUR HUMAN DEVELOPMENT GROUPS

The inequalities in HDI between the four human development groups will be in this chapter complemented with the analysis of inequalities between countries within a given HD group.

Figures 10-13 are showing time distances comparing the level of HDI of individual country with the respective average HDI for a given group for levels that were attained in the period 1980-2012 in each of the groups. Time matrices for all four HD groups and the respective matrices of S-time-step are too large to be adequately presented in the book format. However, these results could be obtained in the electronic form at the Gaptimer web page (link is available in Appendix A2).

These figures present the important overview in terms of time distance inequalities within each group that can be also a rich source of information for comparison between countries of users' interest. The general conclusion is that the disparities in HDI within the analysed HD groups are also large.

Time distance inequalities within the very high HD group

In the very high group in the Figure 10 the largest time lead from the benchmark of the average value for the group is shown by Norway, Australia, and United States with time lead of about 13 years. On the other hand, at the lower level Argentina, Latvia, Croatia, and Seychelles are lagging the average of the very high group for HDI for about 23 years. Interesting information can be obtained also about the trends of S-time-distance over time from the group average for individual countries. For example, the time lead for Norway and Sweden is increasing over time and decreasing for United States, Canada, and Switzerland. Approximately we can say that the range between the Norway and Croatia shows that HDI for Croatia is about 16 percent lower and Croatia is lagging behind Norway for about 32 years.

HDI Level	0.78	0.79	0.80	0.81	0.82	0.83	0.84	0.85	0.86	0.87	0.88	0.89	0.90
Very high group	0	0	0	0	0	0	0	0	0	0	0	0	0
Norway				-7	-7	-7	-7	-7	-7	-8	-9	-10	-13
Australia									-17	-15	-13	-12	-14
United States								-15	-14	-13	-12	-11	-12
Netherlands			-6	-6	-6	-5	-5	-5	-5	-5	-5	-6	-4
Germany	5	4	3	3	2	1	1	0	0	-1	-1	-2	-5
Ireland	6	6	5	4	3	2	1	0	-1	-2	-3	-3	-6
New Zealand				-7	-6	-4	-4	-4	-4	-4	-4	-5	-6
Sweden			-4	-3	-2	-2	-2	-3	-4	-5	-6	-7	-10
Switzerland				-10	-7	-5	-4	-4	-4	-3	-3	-2
Canada					-11	-11	-10	-10	-8	-6	-5	-6
Japan		-3	-4	-4	-4	-4	-4	-3	-3	-3	-2	-2	-4
Iceland	1	1	1	1	0	0	0	0	-1	-1	-1	-2	-1
Korea (Rep. of)	12	11	10	8	7	6	6	5	4	4	3	2	0
Hong Kong (SAR)	7	7	8	10	10	9	8	8	7	6	4	3	1
Denmark		-4	-2	-1	0	0	0	0	0	0	-1	-1	1
Israel	0	1	1	2	1	1	1	1	1	1	1	1	3
Belgium	1	1	1	0	0	-1	-1	-2	-2	-3	-4	1
Slovenia								5	4	3	3	4
Austria	5	5	4	4	4	4	4	4	5	5	4	4
France	8	7	6	5	5	4	4	3	3	3	3	4
Singapore	12	11	10	9	9	8	8	8	8	7	6	5
Finland	2	3	4	4	4	4	4	4	3	3	2	5
Spain	11	10	9	8	6	6	5	4	5	5	6
Italy	10	9	9	8	7	7	6	6	5	5	7
Liechtenstein											7
United Kingdom	7	7	7	6	6	5	5	5	5	7
Luxembourg	6	5	4	4	3	3	2	2	1	8
Czech Republic						8	8	7	6	8
Greece	11	11	11	12	10	9	8	7	13
Brunei Darussalam	7	8	8	7	7	7	8	9
Cyprus	9	10	11	13	15	15	14
Malta	14	14	14	13	13	15	15
Andorra							15
Estonia	17	17	15	14	13	12	16
Slovakia	17	17	16	16	15	14	17
UAE					18	14
Qatar	15	14	14	13	13	18
Hungary	17	16	16	15	14	18
Barbados	15	16	20	20	18
Poland	19	19	19	19	21
Portugal	18	19	20	19
Chile	22	22	21	21
Lithuania	21	20	19	22
Argentina	24	24	23	23
Latvia	22	21	20	23
Croatia	22	22	23
Seychelles	23	23	24
S-time-distance (years):		(-) time lead,			(+) time lag		from benchmark group average						

FIGURE 10 S-time-distance in years as a time measure of the gap of countries from the very high HD group average for a given level of the HDI

SOURCE: Own calculations based on data from Human Development Report 2013, UNDP (2013a).

Time distance inequalities within the high HD group

In the high HD group Bahrain and Kuwait are showing a time lead of 14 years, while the lowest countries in the group Algeria, Sri Lanka, and Tunisia are behind group average for only 8 years. The within group inequalities are lower than in the VHHD group; the range between the Bahrain and Tunisia shows that HDI for Tunisia is about 11 percent lower and Tunisia is lagging behind Bahrain for about 22 years. For countries with empty rows in Figures 11-13 their HDI values are higher than the highest value for the respective group average. The corresponding time matrices to study details are mentioned in Appendix A2.

HDI Level	0.61	0.62	0.63	0.64	0.65	0.66	0.67	0.68	0.69	0.70	0.71	0.72	0.73	0.74	0.75
High group	0	0	0	0	0	0	0	0	0	0	0	0	0	0	0
Bahrain					-8	-9	-10	-11	-12	-13	-13	-13	-13	-13	-14
Bahamas															
Montenegro															
Belarus													-1	-2	-3
Uruguay							-12	-11	-10	-9	-9	-9	-8	-8	-4
Palau															
Kuwait										-18	-14	-13	-13	-13	-14
Romania											-2	-3	-3	-4	-5
Russian Federation												-3	-4	-4	-5
Bulgaria								-14	-13	-12	-9	-5	-4	-5	-5
Saudi Arabia	4	3	2	1	1	0	-1	-2	-3	-3	-4	-4	-4	-4	-4
Cuba			-4	-4	-4	-5	-6	-6	1	0	0	-1	-1	-2	-4
Panama			-5	-4	-3	-3	-4	-5	-5	-5	-5	-4	-4	-4	
Mexico	1	1	1	1	0	0	-1	-2	-4	-4	-4	-5	-4	-3	-4
Libya													5	4	2
Costa Rica			-3	-2	-2	-2	-2	-2	-2	-2	-2	-1	-1	-1	0
Grenada															
Serbia													-5	-4	-5
Malaysia	6	5	4	4	3	2	1	0	-2	-2	-3	-3	-3	-3	-3
Trinidad and Tobago								-16	-6	-4	-2	-2	-2	-2	-3
Antigua and Barbuda															
Kazakhstan							7	5	4	2	2	1	1	2	2
Dominica													-2	0	
Albania							-1	-1	-1	-1	-1	-1	0	0	
Venezuela (Bolivarian Rep. of)			-3	5	7	8	8	7	6	5	4	3	2	1	
Saint Kitts and Nevis														2	
Lebanon												2	2	2	
Iran (Islamic Republic of)	15	14	13	12	11	10	9	8	7	5	5	4	4	3	
Georgia												2	2	4	
Peru	7	7	7	7	6	6	5	4	4	4	4	4	4	4	
Ukraine								5	3	2	2	1	4	5	
T.F.Y.R. Macedonia												3	2	5	
Bosnia and Herzegovina													1		
St. Vincent and the Grenadines													3		
Mauritius	7	6	6	6	6	6	5	4	3	3	3	3	4		
Azerbaijan													4		
Oman												6	4	6	
Jamaica		0	1	2	3	4	4	4	5	6	5	3	6		
Brazil	12	11	10	9	9	8	7	6	5	4	5	5	6		
Armenia			6	9	11	10	9	7	6	5	4	5			
Saint Lucia													5		
Ecuador	3	3	4	5	7	9	9	8	8	7	5	6			
Turkey	14	14	13	12	12	11	10	8	7	6	7	7			
Colombia	11	11	10	10	10	9	9	9	7	7	7				
Algeria	17	16	16	15	13	12	11	9	8	8	8				
Sri Lanka	9	10	10	10	11	10	9	8	8	8	8				
Tunisia	15	15	14	13	12	11	10	9	8	7	9				
S-time-distance (years):				(-) time lead,			(+) time lag			from benchmark group average					

FIGURE 11 S-time-distance in years as a time measure of the gap of countries from the high HD group average for a given level of the HDI

SOURCE: Own calculations based on data from Human Development Report 2013, UNDP (2013a).

Time distance inequalities within the medium HD group

The medium group shows the highest range of the average HDI level in the analysed period, from 0.42 to 0.64, which was visually shown in Figure 5 as the largest increase in HDI between the four HD groups. The largest time lead is shown for Belize of 26 years and Fiji of 17 years. For South Africa there is a clear downward trend from good positions earlier to the average level of the group. Cambodia, Lao, Swaziland, and Bhutan are lagging behind the group average for about 13 years which is considerably less than the time lag for the lowest countries in the very high and in the low group.

HDI Level	0.42	0.43	0.44	0.45	0.46	0.47	0.48	0.49	0.50	0.51	0.52	0.53	0.54	0.55	0.56	0.57	0.58	0.59	0.60	0.61	0.62	0.63	0.64
Medium group	0	0	0	0	0	0	0	0	0	0	0	0	0	0	0	0	0	0	0	0	0	0	0
Tonga																							
Belize																						-27	-26
Samoa																							
Fiji																-22	-21	-19	-18	-17	-17	-17	
Dominican Rep.												-16	-16	-16	-15	-15	-15	-14	-13	-13	-12	-12	-12
Jordan													-19	-18	-17	-16	-16	-15	-14	-14	-13	-14	
China	1	1	0	0	-1	-1	-2	-2	-2	-3	-3	-4	-4	-4	-5	-5	-5	-5	-5	-5	-5	-6	-7
Turkmenistan																							
Thailand								-11	-12	-12	-12	-12	-12	-13	-13	-12	-12	-11	-11	-10	-9	-9	-10
Maldives																			-5	-5	-5	-6	-7
Suriname																							
Gabon												-17	-17	-17	-17	-17	-17	-17	-17	-17	-13	-9	-10
El Salvador							-8	-8	-8	-7	-7	-7	-7	-8	-8	-8	-8	-8	-8	-8	-8	-8	-9
Bolivia								-11	-11	-11	-11	-11	-11	-11	-11	-11	-10	-10	-9	-9	-8	-8	-8
Paraguay														-20	-18	-15	-13	-12	-10	-9	-8	-7	-7
Mongolia															-9	-2	-3	-3	-3	-3	-4	-4	-5
Palestine, State of																							
Egypt	1	1	0	0	-1	-2	-2	-3	-3	-3	-4	-4	-5	-5	-5	-5	-5	-5	-5	-4	-4	-4	-5
Moldova																			-5	-5	-5	-6	-6
Philippines																-18	-14	-12	-10	-7	-6	-5	-4
Uzbekistan																					-3	-3	-3
Syrian Arab Rep.										-13	-12	-12	-12	-11	-11	-9	-8	-7	-5	-4	-2	-2	-3
Micronesia																							-1
Botswana				-5	-6	-7	-8	-8	-9	-10	-11	-11	-12	-13	-13	-14	-14	-4	-2	-1	-1	-1	
Guyana										-3	-3	-4	-4	-4	-4	-4	-4	-3	-3	-2	0	1	
Honduras					-6	-6	-6	-6	-6	-6	-6	-5	-4	-3	-2	-1	1	1	1	0	-1	1	
South Africa																-23	-22	-21	-20	0	1		
Kiribati																					2		
Indonesia		0	0	0	0	0	0	0	1	1	1	1	1	1	1	2	2	2	2	2	2		
Vanuatu																					2		
Kyrgyzstan																		-3	-1	0	2		
Tajikistan												3	2	2	2	1	3	2	2	2	3		
Viet Nam			7	6	6	5	4	4	4	3	3	2	2	2	2	2	2	2	3	3			
Namibia																-1	1	2	3				
Nicaragua						-3	0	1	1	2	2	3	3	2	2	2	3	4					
Morocco	7	7	7	6	6	6	6	6	6	5	5	5	4	4	4	4	5	6					
Iraq																5	7	7					
Cape Verde														3	4	4	5	6					
Guatemala			-1	1	2	3	3	3	3	4	4	4	4	5	5	4	7						
Timor-Leste	20	20	19	19	18	17	16	15	14	12	11	10	9	9	8								
Equatorial Guinea										8	8	9	9	9	11								
India	12	12	12	13	13	13	12	12	11	11	11	10	10	11									
Ghana	8	9	10	12	13	13	13	14	14	13	12	12	11	11									
Cambodia			16	15	14	13	13	12	12	11	12	13											
Lao P. Dem. Rep.	15	15	15	15	14	14	13	13	13	13	13	12	13										
Swaziland										12	11	12											
Bhutan												14											

S-time-distance (years):   (-) time lead,   (+) time lag   from benchmark group average

FIGURE 12 S-time-distance in years as a time measure of the gap of countries from the medium HD group average for a given level of the HDI

SOURCE: Own calculations based on data from Human Development Report 2013, UNDP (2013a).

Time distance inequalities within the low HD group

The low group shows considerable within group inequalities. Figure 13 shows interesting change of positions for several countries over the period. Kenya, Cameron, Togo, Haiti, and Côte d'Ivoire have all decreased their good relative position against group average earlier in the period. Ten countries in the group are lagging behind the group HDI average for more than 20 years. The overall range within the low group can be approximated by the difference between Congo and Niger. The percentage difference in 2012 shows that the HDI level of Niger is about 43 percent lower than that of Congo, which is the highest positioned country in the low group.

Time distance between these two countries is difficult to assess, but it need to be much more than 32 years. There are no entries for Congo (Dem. Rep.) and Niger as their HDI values in the observed three decades have not yet reached the lowest average HDI value of 0.32 for the low group.

HDI Level	0.32	0.33	0.34	0.35	0.36	0.37	0.38	0.39	0.40	0.41	0.42	0.43	0.44	0.45	0.46
Low group	0	0	0	0	0	0	0	0	0	0	0	0	0	0	0
Congo															
Solomon Islands															
Sao Tome and Principe															
Pakistan			-6	-7	-8	-9	-9	-9	-7	-6	-4	-5	-5	-6	-7
Kenya												-24	-23	-8	-7
Bangladesh	0	-1	-1	-2	-3	-4	-6	-7	-7	-6	-6	-6	-6	-6	-6
Angola							2	2	2	2	2	1	0	-2	-3
Myanmar	11	9	7	6	4	3	1	0	0	-1	-1	-1	-1	-2	-3
Cameroon							-17	-18	-17	-17	-16	-6	-5	-4	-3
Madagascar												-5	-5	-5	-6
Lesotho												1	1	1	2
Tanzania (United Rep. of)					2	4	4	3	4	4	4	3	2	1	-1
Nigeria													-1	-1	0
Senegal		-3	-3	-4	-5	-5	-5	-5	-3	-3	-2	-2	-2	-2	-2
Mauritania			-7	-4	-2	-4	-5	-5	-5	-5	-4	-3	-2	-2	-1
Papua New Guinea		-3	-4	-4	-5	-5	-6	-6	-5	-4	-3	-1	0	0	1
Yemen	12	11	9	7	5	4	2	1	0	0	0	-1	0	0	1
Nepal	7	5	3	2	0	-1	-2	-2	-2	-2	-1	-1	0	0	1
Togo					-12	-11	-9	-9	-8	-7	-6	-4	-1	1	
Haiti			-6	-8	-9	-10	-12	-12	-11	-8	-5	-3	-1	2	
Uganda	11	9	8	6	5	4	2	2	2	2	2	2	2	2	
Zambia							2	2	3	4	4	3	4		
Djibouti										3	3	4	4		
Gambia	8	8	7	7	7	8	8	7	5	4	3	3	4		
Benin	9	8	7	5	4	3	1	1	1	1	3	4			
Rwanda	19	17	15	13	11	9	7	5	5	5	5	5			
Côte d'Ivoire				-8	-3	-3	-2	-1	1	3	4	6			
Zimbabwe				18	16	14	12	11	-7	-10	-13				
Comoros											1				
Sudan	12	10	9	8	7	5	5	4	5	6					
Malawi	13	12	11	10	11	10	8	7	7	7					
Ethiopia	24	22	19	17	15	13	11	10							
Liberia	25	23	20	18	16	15	12								
Afghanistan	23	21	19	18	16	15									
Guinea-Bissau					16	17									
Guinea			20	20											
Burundi	25	24	22	21											
Sierra Leone	24	23	22	21											
Central African Republic	26	24	22	22											
Eritrea				22											
Mali	25	23	22												
Burkina Faso	26	25	24												
Chad	26	25	25												
Mozambique	29														
Congo (Dem. Rep. of the)															
Niger															

S-time-distance (years):   (-) time lead,   (+) time lag   from benchmark group average

FIGURE 13 S-time-distance in years as a time measure of the gap of countries from the low HD group average for a given level of the HDI
SOURCE: Own calculations based on data from Human Development Report 2013, UNDP (2013a).

An overview of different perception of inequality based on percentage and time distance measures for HDI

Following the example of Table 1 for different measures of inequalities in life expectancy, Table 2 presents the three measures of inequality for the HDI. In the first three rows the three measures of differences between average values of HDI for the four human development groups are presented. Again, the perception of the degree of inequality between static measures and time distance can be rather different.

Average value of HDI for the high (HHD) development group is the percentage terms about 16 percent lower than that of the very high group (VHHD), while the time distance has been more than 32 years, which is indicating a rather long period of time that there was no similarity in the level of the HDI for the two groups. Between the averages for the next two groups (HHD and MHD) the percentage amounted to about 16 percent with time distance of about a quarter a century. The difference between the medium and low group (MHD and LHD) is larger in percentage terms (about 27 percent) and slightly lower in time distance of about 23 years. The reason why at higher percentage difference the time distance is smaller (though still high) comes about from the dynamic characteristics of HDI development in the two respective groups. Namely, measured by S-time-step the growth of HDI in the last five steps was highest in the low group and thus making the time distance dimension of the inequality lower.

Comparison		Absolute difference	Percentage difference	S-time-distance (years)
Differences between groups				
	VHHD - HHD	0.147	16.2%	> 32
	HHD - MHD	0.118	15.6%	25
	MHD - LHD	0.174	27.2%	23
	VHHD-LHD	0.439	48.5%	> 80
Differences within groups				
Group				
VHHD	Norway-Croatia	0.150	15.7%	32
HHD	Bahrain-Tunisia	0.084	10.6%	22
MHD	China-Bhutan	0.161	23.0%	18
LHD	Congo-Niger	0.230	43.1%	> 32
	Norway-Niger	0.651	68.2%	> 104

TABLE 2 Different perception of inequality based on percentage and time distance measures for HDI
SOURCE: Own calculations based on data from Human Development Report 2013, UNDP (2013a).

If one looks at differences between averages for the very high and the low group (VHHD and LHD), i.e. over the range of all HD groups the assessment of the degree of disparity shows that the average for the low group is about 49 percent lower than that of the very high group. In other words, the two measures of the degree of inequality over the range of these groups is in percentage terms about 50 percent and in time distance dimension can be approximated as more than 80 years.

The percentage difference indicates that the average value of HDI for the very high group is nearly 2 times higher than that of the low group. While this is high it does not show a very high degree of inequality when one compares that for GNI per capita in PPP terms (constant 2005 international $) which shows that the average GNI per capita is more than 20 (twenty!) times higher (UNDP, 2013b) for the very high group (not to mention even much higher relative differences with some high income countries). Time distance assessment about 82 years seems to be a much more realistic assessment of the degree of inequality in HDI.

The second part of Table 2 shows the differences in HDI between countries within the four development groups, which will show higher degree of inequalities between countries than that between groups. If we approximate the degree of inequality between Norway and Niger, in percentage terms HDI for Niger is about 68 percent lower than that of Norway and in time distance dimension the degree of inequality is approximated by the time delay of more than 104 years. The largest differences between countries are in the low group where the percentage difference between the highest and the lowest end of the group (represented by Congo and Niger) amounts to 43 percent. The time distance is difficult to estimate, a rough assessment is considerably larger than 32 years. The next highest degree of inequality within a given group in terms of time distance is between Norway and Croatia in the very high group amounting to 32 years.

Let us illustrate that difference of perception of the degree of inequality in the case of Nepal, which was in terms of HDI in the last years at about the average value for the low group. We can show their position in life expectancy and GDP per capita over a long period of time by comparing it with long time series for Sweden. For life expectancy the value for Nepal was about 15 percent lower than that of Sweden, while the time distance was 66 years. For GDP per capita (Maddison, 2010) the value for Nepal is about 95 percent lower (being about 5 percent of value for Sweden only) and the time distance was 140 years. For HDI there is no time series long enough to estimate the time distance of Nepal to the best countries. Static difference between Sweden and Nepal shows that HDI for Nepal is about 50 percent lower than that of Sweden. A rough and ready estimate of time distance may be built from time distance of Nepal behind China of about 26 years, time distance of China behind Argentina of 24 years, and time distance of Argentina behind Sweden of 25 years. Such rough estimate of time distance in the neighbourhood of around 75 years gives a different perception of the inequality than the percentage difference.

It seems that we can conclude in the same way, as it was shown for the inequalities in the life expectancy in Table 1, that also for the HDI the static differences in percentage terms in many cases appear to be small while the time distance dimension gives a very different perception of the magnitude of the gap.

Chapter 6

DISPARITIES WITHIN EU 27

As mentioned in the previous chapter time matrices for all four HD groups and the respective matrices of S-time-step are too large to be adequately presented in the book format. Therefore we have chosen to use the HDI results for EU27 countries to show how the time matrix format can be used for a group of countries which is smaller than the HD groups in UNDP Report.

Figure 14 shows the results for the period 1980-2012 with the range of HDI between 0.70 and 0.92, which is very similar to the time matrix for the VHHD group, only Norway, Australia, and the United States went beyond 0.92. In the EU27 time matrix three countries had at the beginning of the period values lower than 0.70, which were left out in Figure 14 to make it smaller.

HDI level	0.70	0.71	0.72	0.73	0.74	0.75	0.76	0.77	0.78	0.79	0.80	0.81	0.82	0.83	0.84	0.85	0.86	0.87	0.88	0.89	0.90	0.91	0.92
Netherlands											1980	1983	1985	1987	1990	1992	1994	1996	1998	2000	2005	2007	**2011**
Germany					1980	1982	1983	1985	1986	1988	1990	1991	1993	1994	1996	1997	1999	2000	2002	2003	2005	2008	**2012**
Ireland						1981	1983	1985	1987	1989	1991	1992	1993	1994	1995	1997	1998	1999	2000	2002	2004	**2006**	
Sweden											1983	1986	1989	1991	1992	1993	1995	1996	1997	1998	2000	**2010**	
Denmark										1980	1984	1988	1991	1993	1995	1996	1998	2000	2002	2004	**2011**		
Belgium							1981	1983	1985	1987	1989	1990	1992	1993	1995	1996	1998	1999	**2007**				
Austria						1981	1983	1985	1987	1989	1991	1993	1995	1996	1998	2001	2003	2005	2007	**2010**			
France				1980	1982	1984	1986	1988	1989	1991	1992	1994	1995	1997	1998	2000	2001	2004	2006	**2010**			
Slovenia																2001	2003	2004	2006	**2009**			
Finland								1981	1984	1987	1990	1992	1994	1997	1999	2001	2002	2003	2005	**2010**			
Spain	1980	1982	1984	1986	1987	1989	1990	1992	1993	1994	1995	1996	1997	1998	1999	2001	2004	2006	**2009**				
Italy				1981	1984	1986	1988	1990	1991	1993	1995	1996	1998	2000	2001	2002	2004	2005	**2010**				
UK						1981	1983	1986	1989	1991	1993	1995	1996	1998	2000	2002	2004	**2008**					
Luxembourg						1981	1982	1984	1986	1987	1989	1991	1992	1994	1995	1997	1998	2000	**2009**				
Czech Rep.															2001	2002	2003	2005	**2009**				
Greece					1981	1983	1985	1987	1990	1992	1995	1997	2000	2001	2002	2003	2004	**2012**					
Cyprus			1981	1982	1984	1985	1987	1989	1990	1994	1997	2001	2006	2007	**2009**								
Malta				1982	1984	1986	1988	1991	1993	1995	1998	2000	2002	2004	2007	**2010**							
Estonia					1990	1992	1994	1996	1997	1999	2000	2002	2003	2004	2005	**2010**							
Slovakia							1992	1995	1998	2001	2003	2004	2006	2007	**2012**								
Hungary		1982	1991	1992	1993	1995	1996	1997	1999	2000	2002	2003	2005	**2011**									
Poland											2001	2003	2006	2008	**2012**								
Lithuania					1993	1998	2000	2002	2003	2004	2005	**2010**											
Portugal	1988	1989	1991	1992	1994	1995	1997	1998	2000	2003	2006	**2008**											
Latvia	1990	1993	1995	1998	2000	2001	2002	2003	2004	2005	2006	**2011**											
Romania		2000	2001	2002	2003	2004	2006	2007	**2008**														
Bulgaria	1989	1994	1999	2001	2003	2004	2006	2008	**2011**														

FIGURE 14 Time matrix for HDI for EU27 countries (1980-2012)
SOURCE: Own calculations based on data from Human Development Report 2013, UNDP (2013a).

As indicated in the analysis in Chapter 5 for the four HD groups the disparities in Human Development Index are also large within EU27 countries. The largest difference is between Netherlands and Bulgaria, the absolute difference in HDI is 0.139, in percentage terms Bulgaria is 15.1 percent lower than Netherlands, and the time distance was more than 32 years. Similar results are shown also for Romania, for Latvia the corresponding values are 0.107, 11.6 percent, and S-time-distance around 29 years.

Comparisons of S-time-distances for HDI for EU27 countries and average of the very high HD group

LEVEL	0.78	0.79	0.80	0.81	0.82	0.83	0.84	0.85	0.86	0.87	0.88	0.89	0.90
Very high group	0	0	0	0	0	0	0	0	0	0	0	0	0
Netherlands			-6	-6	-6	-5	-5	-5	-5	-5	-5	-6	-4
Germany	5	4	3	3	2	1	1	0	0	-1	-1	-2	-5
Ireland	6	6	5	4	3	2	1	0	-1	-2	-3	-3	-6
Sweden			-4	-3	-2	-2	-2	-3	-4	-5	-6	-7	-10
Denmark		-4	-2	-1	0	0	0	0	0	0	-1	-1	1
Belgium	1	1	1	0	0	-1	-1	-2	-2	-3	-4	1	
Austria	5	5	4	4	4	4	4	4	5	5	4	4	
France	8	7	6	5	5	4	4	3	3	3	3	4	
Slovenia								5	4	3	3	4	
Finland	2	3	4	4	4	4	4	4	3	3	2	5	
Spain	11	10	9	8	6	6	5	4	5	5	6		
Italy	10	9	9	8	7	7	6	6	5	5	7		
United Kingdom	7	7	7	6	6	5	5	5	5	7			
Luxembourg	6	5	4	4	3	3	2	2	1	8			
Czech Republic						8	8	7	6	8			
Greece	11	11	11	12	10	9	8	7	13				
Cyprus	9	10	11	13	15	15	14						
Malta	14	14	14	13	13	15	15						
Estonia	17	17	15	14	13	12	16						
Slovakia	17	17	16	16	15	14	17						
Hungary	17	16	16	15	14	18							
Poland	19	19	19	19	21								
Lithuania	21	20	19	22									
Portugal	18	19	20	19									
Latvia	22	21	20	23									
Romania	26												
Bulgaria	29												

S-time-distance (years):   (-) time lead,   (+) time lag   from benchmark very high group

FIGURE 15 S-time-distance in years as a time measure of the gap of EU27 countries from very high human development group (VHHD)
SOURCE: Own calculations based on data from Human Development Report 2013, UNDP (2013a).

Figure 15 shows the time distances against the average of the VHHD as the benchmark (not against the EU27 average). Four EU27 countries are ahead of the average for the VHHD group; these are Netherlands, Germany, Ireland, and Sweden, while Denmark and Belgium have at the end of the period lost their advantage against the average of VHHD group. Austria, France, and Slovenia are less than five years behind this benchmark, while the time lag for six EU27 countries is more than 20 years.

EU27 countries with respect to the HDI were in the very high human development group occupying positions from 4 to 44 in the world ranking, with the exception of Romania and Bulgaria that fell in the high human development group, occupying positions 56 and 57. Of the first ten EU27 countries Netherlands, Germany, Ireland, and Sweden are also in the first 10 countries in the world rankings; Denmark, Belgium, Austria had world ranks below 20; France occupied rank 20, and Slovenia and Finland rank 21. In non-income HDI the EU27 countries the ranking is different. The best five EU27 countries were positioned in the world table Ireland at rank 4, Germany rank 7, Netherlands rank 8, Sweden rank 12, and Slovenia rank 13.

The smaller group of EU27 countries can be used as one example how analyses as in Chapter 3 and 4 could be performed also among selected countries within geographical regions, neighbouring countries, countries at the similar level of development or policy orientations, etc. From the time matrix format of the HDI results for four HD groups, which are provided in the electronic form at the Gaptimer web page (link is available in Appendix A2) one can select any number of countries for such comparisons depending on the interest of the user.

Comparing the HDI position of five Central European countries with very high HD group and among themselves

Here the example is provided of the HDI position of five EU countries, i.e. Slovenia and four neighbouring countries, Austria, Italy, Hungary, and Croatia. The time matrix of the four indices is presented in Figure 16. In general the component indices follow the same order than in the very high HD group in Figure 9: the highest level is that of health index, followed by education and income indices. The only exception is Austria, where the income index is higher than education index.

From the five countries the highest HDI positions are those of Austria and Slovenia, so we have ordered countries in the same way for component indices. In the time matrix shown Slovenia has even reached the level of HDI at 0.89 earlier than Austria, but by the HDI levels rounded to three decimal places in the UNDP Statistical Annex, 2012 Austria value is higher.

Figure 16 is the time matrix format of visualisation as in earlier examples, i.e. times when a given level of the corresponding index was attained. Figures 15 and 17 show two ways of presenting the HDI situation for the five countries in the time distance perspective. The S-time-distances from the average values for the very high HD group as the benchmark are presented in Figure 15. S-time-distances in Figure 17 are calculated in a different way. Firstly, data as rounded in the UNDP Statistical Annex to three decimal places were used for this calculation, in contrast to the two decimal places in time matrices to make the number of positions manageable in visualisation. Secondly, for each index the actual yearly values were calculated against the trend for the benchmark.

Country	HDI					Health index					Education index					Income index				
	Austria	Slovenia	Italy	Hungary	Croatia	Austria	Slovenia	Italy	Hungary	Croatia	Austria	Slovenia	Italy	Hungary	Croatia	Austria	Slovenia	Italy	Hungary	Croatia
0.97								2008												
0.96						2011		2005												
0.95						2008		2003												
0.94						2005		2000												
0.93						2003	2009	1998				2007								
0.92						2001	2007	1996				2005								
0.91						1999	2005	1993				2004								
0.90						1996	2003	1991				2003								
0.89	2010	2009				1994	2002	1988		2010		2002		2012						
0.88	2007	2006	2010			1991	2000	1986		2007		2001		2005						
0.87	2005	2004	2005			1989	1998	1984		2003		2000		2004		2011				
0.86	2003	2003	2004			1987	1995	1982	2012	1999		1999		2002		2006				
0.85	2001	2001	2002			1985	1993		2009	1997	2009	1998	2010	2001		2001				
0.84	1998		2001			1982	1991		2005	1995	2008	1997	2007	2000		1997				
0.83	1996		2000	2011		1980	1988		2003	1992	2007	1996	2006	1999		1994		2008		
0.82	1995		1998	2005			1985		2001	1990	2006	1995	2005	1999		1991	2008	1996		
0.81	1993		1996	2003			1982		1998	1986	2005	1994	2004	1998		1988	2012	1992		
0.80	1991		1995	2002	2009				1996	1981	2003	1993	2004	1998		1985	2004	1988		
0.79	1989		1993	2000	2006				1993		2001	1992	2003	1997		1981	2002	1985		
0.78	1987		1991	1999	2004				1991		1999	1991	2002	1997	2010			1982		
0.77	1985		1990	1997	2002						1998		2002	1996	2008					
0.76	1983		1988	1996	2001						1997		2001	1996	2006					
0.75	1981		1986	1995	1999						1995		2000	1995	2004				2012	2009
0.74			1984	1993	1996						1994		1999	1994	2003				2003	2005
0.73			1981	1992	1994						1993		1999	1994	2002				2002	2004
0.72				1991	1991						1991		1998	1993	2002				2000	2002
0.71				1982							1990		1997	1993	2001				1988	2000
0.70											1988		1996	1992	2000				1982	
0.69											1987		1995	1992	1998					
0.68											1986		1994	1991	1997					
0.67											1984		1993	1991	1996					
0.66											1983		1992	1990	1995					
0.65											1981		1991		1993					
0.64											1980		1990		1992					
0.63													1989		1991					
0.62													1987							
0.61													1986							
0.60													1984							
0.59													1982							
0.58													1981							

FIGURE 16 A quick visual overview of trends 1980-2012 for five Central European countries: time when a given indicator level was attained
SOURCE: Own calculations based on data from UNDP (2013b).

The values of S-time-distance in Figure 17 are thus slightly different than those in Figure 15 due to different levels of comparison and rounding, but this does not affect the general conclusions. The time lags behind the average of the very high HD group in 2012 were slightly higher for these five EU countries than in 2008 before the crisis, thus mainly due to the income component. For income index Hungary and Croatia are even more than 32 years behind the VHHD benchmark. It is interesting that by component indices there are cases where some of these five countries are better that the average for the very high HD group: for the health index Italy had a time lead of about 10 years and Austria of 5 years, for education index Slovenia was about 8 years ahead, and for income index Austria with the time lead of about 7 years.

Time	HDI					Health index					Education index					Income index				
	Austria	Slovenia	Italy	Hungary	Croatia	Austria	Slovenia	Italy	Hungary	Croatia	Austria	Slovenia	Italy	Hungary	Croatia	Austria	Slovenia	Italy	Hungary	Croatia
1980																				
1990	5					0		-5			9					-2		2		
2000	4	5	7	16		-1	9	-7		14	8	-1	14	1		-3	19	4		
2005	5	3	5	14	22	-2	5	-7		16	10	-3	9	1	17	-3	17	7		
2006	4	3	4	14	22	-3	4	-7		15	10	-4	9	2	17	-2	16	7		
2007	4	2	5	15	21	-3	4	-8	26	16	10	-4	9	3	17	-2	14	8		
2008	4	2	5	16	22	-3	4	-8	26	16	10	-5	9	3	18	-3	14	10		
2009	4	4	7	17	23	-4	4	-8	26	15	9	-5	10	4	19	-7	19	15		
2010	4	4	7	18	23	-4	4	-9	26	16	9	-6	10	5	18	-6	20	15		
2011	5	5	8	18	24	-5	4	-9	26	16	10	-7	11	6	19	-6	21	16		
2012	5	6	9	19	25	-5	4	-10	26	16	11	-8	12	7	20	-7	23	18	> 32	> 32

S-time-distance (years):　　　(-) time lead,　　(+) time lag　　from very high HD group

FIGURE 17 S-time-distance in years as a time measure of the gap from average of the very high HD group as the benchmark

SOURCE: Own calculations based on data from UNDP (2013b).

Slightly different results are obtained if S-time-distances are calculated against the leading country from the five countries as the benchmark for each component index. Between the five countries for HDI the leading country is Austria, behind it Slovenia with a lag of two years, Italy 5 years, Hungary about 15 years and Croatia about 20 years. In health index Italy is leading for about 6 years ahead of Austria, about 12 years ahead of Slovenia, 22 from Croatia and 30 years ahead of Hungary. For education index the leading country is Slovenia, Hungary is lagging for 10 years, Austria and Italy around 13 years, and Croatia about 21 years. In income index Austria is clearly in the lead, Italy lagging 20 years, Slovenia around 25 years, while Hungary and Croatia are lagging behind by more than 32 years.

Thus even for neighbouring countries the S-time-distances show substantial differences in time as another picture of reality. Two groups of countries in the next two chapters will add to this example.

Chapter 7

BRICS COUNTRIES

Comparisons of disparities in the human development indices are extended to BRICS countries. Time matrix in Figure 18 provides a quick visual overview for these countries for four indices: HDI, health, education, and income index. For HDI the rank is clear: Russia is followed by Brazil, China, South Africa, and India. The S-time-distances for HDI amounted to 10 years of time lag of Brazil behind Russia, 6 years of China behind of Brazil, 7 years of South Africa behind China, and more than 32 years of India behind South Africa. With respect to the world rank for HDI in 2012 the BRICS countries Russia occupies rank 55, Brazil rank 85 (both in high HD group), China rank 101, South Africa rank 121, and India rank 136 (all three in medium HD group).

For all four indices the progress is shown by the increases except for the health index for South Africa where the index value decreased in the part of the period. The relative position of countries within the three component indices has been rather different from that in the overall HDI.

The value of the health index is highest in Brazil and China, followed by Russia, India, and South Africa. Russia is behind Brazil for 14 years and behind China for 24 years; India is behind Brazil for 24 years; the present value of health index for South Africa is much lower than in any other BRICS country because of the large decrease from 1990 to about 2006 when the negative trend turned around and the health index started to increase again.

Russia was very much ahead of all other four countries in education index. It is followed by South Africa, Brazil, China, and with a great delay for India; although there was substantial progress in attaining higher values of index over the period in all countries. The interesting point is that in all countries the increase in the value of the education index was more than 0.22, which are the highest increases of all indices with the exception of the income index for China. For education index South Africa is about 21 years behind Russia, the time delay for Brazil is about 24 years, for China about 32 years. The level of education index for India is much lower.

For income index for BRICS countries there were very different dynamics indicated in the analysed period. By far fastest increase was in China where S-time-step showed that increase for one step (0.01) in income index was attained about each 10 months. This is also the highest increase of all indices in Figure 19. The second highest increase in income index was observed in India; however, the S-time-step for one step (0.01) was about 19 months, i.e. India needed in the analysed period about twice the time for such increase as China. China and India showed increasing trends over the whole period. For the other three countries after initial fall in income index Brazil started to increase after 1990, Russia and South Africa after 2000.

Country	HDI					Health index					Education index					Income index				
	Russia	Brazil	China	S.Africa	India	Russia	Brazil	China	S.Africa	India	Russia	Brazil	China	S.Africa	India	Russia	Brazil	China	S.Africa	India
0.86											2009									
0.85											2007									
0.84							2010	2010			2005									
0.83							2008	2007			2004									
0.82							2007	2004			2003									
0.81							2004	2001			2002									
0.80							2002	1997			2002									
0.79							2000	1994			2001									
0.78	2010						1998	1990			2000									
0.77	2007					2011	1997	1987			1998									
0.76	2006					2009	1995	1985			1996									
0.75	2005					2008	1993	1982			1995									
0.74	2003					2006	1992				1993									
0.73	2002	2012				2005	1990				1992					2011				
0.72	2001	2009				2003	1988			2012	1990					2009				
0.71		2007				2000	1987			2010	1989					2006				
0.70		2005					1985			2008	1988			2009		2005				
0.69		2004	2010				1983			2006	1987			2006		2004				
0.68		2002	2009				1982			2004	1986			1999		2003	2011			
0.67		2000	2008				1980			2003	1985	2009		1998		2002	2009		2010	
0.66		1999	2007							2001	1984	2008		1998		2001	2007		2006	
0.65		1998	2006						1990	1999	1983	2006		1997			2004		2004	
0.64		1996	2005						1991	1997	1982	2004		1996			1999	2011	2001	
0.63		1995	2004						1992	1995	1981	2003		1995			1992	2011		
0.62		1994	2003	2010					1993	1993		2003	2009	1994				2010		
0.61		1993	2002	2007					1994	1991		2002	2008	1993				2009		
0.60		1991	2001	1986					1995	1989		2001	2007	1992				2008		
0.59		1990	2000	1984					1996	1987		2000	2006	1992				2007		
0.58		1989	1999	1982					1997	1985		2000	2005	1991				2007		
0.57		1987	1998	1980					1998	1983		1999	2004	1990				2006		
0.56		1986	1997						1999	1981		1998	2003	1989				2006		
0.55		1984			2011				2000			1997	2002	1987				2005		
0.54		1983			2009				2001			1996	2001	1986				2004		
0.53		1981			2008				2002			1996	2000	1985				2004		
0.52					2007				2011			1995	1999	1984				2002		
0.51					2005				2010			1994	1998	1983				2001		2011
0.50					2004				2009			1994	1997	1982				2001		2010
0.49					2003				2007			1993	1996	1980				2000		2009
0.48					2002							1992	1995					1999		2007
0.47					2001							1991	1993					1998		2006
0.46					1999							1991	1992					1997		2005
0.45					1998							1990	1991		2008			1997		2004
0.44					1996							1989	1990		2007			1996		2003
0.43					1994							1988	1989		2006			1996		2002
0.42					1992							1987	1987		2005			1995		2000
0.41					1990							1986	1986		2004			1994		1998
0.40					1988							1986	1984		2003			1994		1997
0.39					1987							1985	1982		2002			1993		1995
0.38					1985							1984	1981		2002			1992		1993
0.37					1984							1983			2001			1991		1991
0.36					1982							1982			1999			1990		1989
0.35					1981							1981			1997			1990		1986
0.34												1980			1995			1989		1984
0.33															1994			1988		1982
0.32															1992			1987		
0.31															1990			1986		
0.30															1989			1985		
0.29															1987			1984		
0.28															1986			1983		
0.27															1985			1982		
0.26															1984			1981		
0.25															1982			1981		
0.24															1981					
0.23															1980					

Only for South Africa among the BRICS countries the health index value decreased.

FIGURE 18 A quick visual overview over BRICS countries (trends 1980-2012): time when a given indicator level was attained

SOURCE: Own calculations based on data from UNDP (2013b).

	HDI					Health index					Education index					Income index				
Country	Russia	Brazil	China	S.Africa	India	Russia	Brazil	China	S.Africa	India	Russia	Brazil	China	S.Africa	India	Russia	Brazil	China	S.Africa	India
0.86											1.5									
0.85											2.1									
0.84							1.9	2.8			1.1									
0.83							1.9	3.0			0.9									
0.82							2.2	3.6			0.9									
0.81							2.3	3.6			0.9									
0.80							2.2	3.6			0.9									
0.79							1.6	3.6			1.0									
0.78	2.6						1.6	2.6			1.6									
0.77	1.1					2.0	1.6	2.6			1.6									
0.76	1.3					1.4	1.6	2.6			1.6									
0.75	1.3					1.2	1.6				1.6									
0.74	1.3					1.1	1.6				1.6									
0.73	1.3	2.9				2.4	1.7				1.6					2.3				
0.72		2.1				2.9	1.7			1.8	1.0					3.3				
0.71		1.8					1.7			1.8	1.0					0.9				
0.70		1.7					1.7			1.8	1.0			2.8		1.1				
0.69		1.7	1.2				1.7			1.8	1.0			6.4		1.1				
0.68		1.7	1.2				1.7			1.9	1.0			0.8		1.1	1.4			
0.67		1.3	1.0							1.9	1.0	1.8		0.9		1.1	2.6			4.5
0.66		1.3	0.8							1.9	1.0	1.8		0.8			2.4			2.0
0.65		1.3	0.8						-0.9	2.0	1.0	1.2		0.9			4.8			2.9
0.64		1.3	1.0						-0.9	2.0	1.0	0.9		0.8			7.1	0.9		
0.63		1.3	1.1						-0.9	2.0		0.9		0.9				0.8		
0.62		1.3	1.1	2.5					-0.9	2.0		1.0	1.1	0.8				0.8		
0.61		1.3	1.1	21.4					-0.9	2.0		0.9	1.1	0.9				0.8		
0.60		1.3	1.1	2.0					-0.9	2.1		0.9	0.9	0.9				0.8		
0.59		1.5	1.1	2.0					-0.9	2.1		0.7	0.7	0.9				0.6		
0.58		1.5	1.1	2.0					-0.9	2.1		0.7	0.9	0.9				0.5		
0.57		1.5	1.1						-0.9	2.1		0.7	1.1	1.2				0.5		
0.56		1.5	1.1						-0.9			0.7	1.1	1.2				0.6		
0.55		1.5	1.1		1.8				-0.9			0.7	1.1	1.2				0.7		
0.54		1.5	1.1		1.4				-0.9			0.7	1.1	1.2				0.8		
0.53			1.1		1.1				-9.7			0.7	1.1	1.2				0.8		
0.52			1.1		1.1				1.2			0.7	1.1	1.2				0.8		
0.51			1.1		1.2				1.3			0.7	1.1	1.2				0.8		1.3
0.50			1.1		1.1				2.3			0.7	1.1	1.2				0.8		0.9
0.49			1.1		1.1							0.7	1.1					0.8		1.5
0.48			1.1		1.1							0.7	1.1					0.8		1.1
0.47			1.1		1.4							0.7	1.1					0.8		0.9
0.46			1.1		1.9							0.7	1.1					0.8		1.2
0.45			1.1		1.9							0.9	1.1		0.8			0.8		1.3
0.44			1.1		1.9							0.9	1.5		0.9			0.8		1.3
0.43			1.1		1.9							0.9	1.5		1.2			0.8		1.3
0.42			1.1		1.9							0.9	1.5		0.9			0.8		1.8
0.41					1.5							0.9	1.5		0.9			0.8		1.9
0.40					1.5							0.9	1.5		0.9			0.8		1.9
0.39					1.5							0.9	1.5		0.9			0.8		1.9
0.38					1.5							0.9			0.9			0.8		1.9
0.37					1.5							0.9			1.2			0.8		2.1
0.36					1.5							0.9			2.0			0.8		2.2
0.35												0.9			2.0			0.9		2.2
0.34															2.0			0.9		2.2
0.33															2.0			0.9		
0.32															1.8			0.9		
0.31															1.2			0.9		
0.30															1.2			0.9		
0.29															1.2			0.9		
0.28															1.2			0.9		
0.27															1.2			0.9		
0.26															1.2			0.9		
0.25															1.2					
0.24															1.2					
0.23																				

Text box (Education index): On the average dynamics in the education index was the highest: 1.2 years per one level (0.01).

Text box (Income index): Highest dynamics is in China: increase for one step (0.01) in income index was attained each 10 months.

Text box (Health index): The group average dynamics in the health index is about 1.8 years per one level (0.01) with slower dynamics for China and unfortunate fall for South Africa.

Text box (HDI): The average dynamics for HDI has been about 1.5 years per one level for Russia, Brasil, and India; better for China and worse for South Africa.

FIGURE 19 A quick visual overview over BRICS countries (trends 1980-2012)
S-time-step: how many years were needed to reach the next level of the indicator
SOURCE: Own calculations based on data from UNDP (2013b).

As far as the levels of income index are concerned, Russia had the highest level followed by Brazil and South Africa and a slightly lower level for China. Russia is about 8 years ahead of Brazil and South Africa, and more years ahead of China which is growing very fast. The level of India is much lower, about 30 percent below the level of Russia. In Figure 19 there is a more detailed figure of calculation of S-time-step showing how many years were needed to reach the next level of the corresponding human development indices. A quick overview shows the average dynamics for HDI has been about 1.5 years per one level for Russia, Brazil, and India; better for China (less) and worse (more years) for South Africa due to negative effect of the health index.

For the three countries (Russia, Brazil, and India) average dynamics in the health index is about 1.8 years per one level (0.01) with slower dynamics for China (about 3 years for one level) and the unfortunate fall for South Africa. The highest dynamics in general was that for the education index (average of S-time-step about 1.2 years) followed by the income index (average 1.4 years with large deviations) and slower dynamics in health index. Within countries, dynamics for China is exceptional for income index, average for education index, and slow for health index.

The BRICS countries include about 3000 millions of people amounting to about 43 percent of the world population. The majority of these countries are positioned in the medium HD group, though China is very fast approaching the lower entry of the high HD group. In this chapter we have indicated some possible comparisons that stem from the time distance presentation across the BRICS countries with very interesting differences both with respect to levels across the component indices as well as their dynamics as presented by S-time-step statistics.

Chapter 8

GULF COORDINATION COUNCIL COUNTRIES

The countries of the Gulf Coordination Council (GCC) are taken as another example of how time distance perspective and time matrix visualisation can provide another dynamic view of the position in the human development advancement. The six countries belong to two HD groups: Qatar and United Arab Emirates (UAE) to the very high, while Bahrain, Kuwait, Saudi Arabia, and Oman to the high HD group. The respective ranks in the world HDI rankings were in 2012 36, 41, for the first two countries, and 48, 54, 57, and 84 for others.

Figure 20 follows the earlier time matrices presenting visualisation of the development in the analysed period 1980-2012 for the HDI and three component indices: Figure 8 for the world view of four HD groups, Figure 16 for five Central European countries and Figure 18 for BRICS countries. The main characteristic of the time matrix for GCC countries is that the highest values for three countries (Qatar, Kuwait, and UAE) are for income index, followed by health index, the lowest values for all six countries are for education index. This ordering is different than in most other three time matrices mentioned, which means that even this decomposition into three sub-indices can indicate substantial differences in the structure of development.

For income index these three countries occupy very prominent ranks in the world rankings: Qatar rank 1, Kuwait 3, and UAE 10. However, for four of the GCC countries there were decreases in the income index during the analysed period. The latest values of the index (which are in time matrices emphasised by the bolding the respective latest years) were the highest values only for Qatar and Oman.

Health index shows higher values than that for income in Bahrain, Saudi Arabia, and Oman, in all countries substantially higher values than that for education. Over the whole analysed period the fastest increase in health index were attained in Saudi Arabia and Oman, where the average S-time-steps were 1.7 years and 1 year for one unit of increase (0.01), though in the last years in Oman this is not increasing any more.

For education the leading countries in the region were Bahrain, Saudi Arabia, and UAE, with values of S-time-step, 0.8 years for UAE and Saudi Arabia, and 0.9 years for Bahrain. This means that on the average these three countries needed less than one year to increase values of the education index for 0.01. In general the education index is both the weakest component in the region as well as with the lowest ranking in the world ranking of all three components.

Index level	Human Development Index						Health Index						Education Index						Income Index					
	Qatar	UAE	Bahrain	Kuwait	Saudi Arabia	Oman	Qatar	UAE	Bahrain	Kuwait	Saudi Arabia	Oman	Qatar	UAE	Bahrain	Kuwait	Saudi Arabia	Oman	Qatar	UAE	Bahrain	Kuwait	Saudi Arabia	Oman
1.00																			**2012**					
0.99																			2011					
0.98																			2010					
0.97																			2009					
0.96																			2001	2006				
0.95																			1999	2006				
0.94																			1997	2007				
0.93																			1995	2008			2007	
0.92							2011												1994	2008			**2011**	
0.91							2007												1992	2009			2002	
0.90							2003												1990	**2009**			1999	
0.89							2000	2010															1996	
0.88							1998	2007															1992	
0.87							1995	2004	2012															
0.86							1992	2001	2007	2011													1980	
0.85							1989	1998	2002	2004	**2011**	2001											1981	
0.84							1987	1996	1997	1998	2008	**2006**											1983	
0.83	**2011**	2006					1985	1993	1992	1991	2005	1996											1984	
0.82	2004	**2009**					1983	1991	1989	1988	2003	1994											1986	
0.81	2002						1981	1989	1986	1985	2000	1992									2006		1987	**2012**
0.80	2000		**2008**					1987	1984	1982	1998	1990									2007	**2012**		2007
0.79	1998		2002	**2012**				1985	1982		1995	1989									2008	2010		2006
0.78	1996		2000	2000	**2011**			1984			1993	1989									**2009**			2003
0.77	1995		1998	1998	2009			1982			1991	1988									1995			2000
0.76	1993		1997	1997	2008			1980			1989	1988									1993			1998
0.75	1991		1995	1996	2006						1988	1987									1992			1995
0.74	1988		1994	1994	2004						1987	1986			2008						1990			1992
0.73	1981		1993	1993	2002	**2012**					1986	1986			2005									1990
0.72			1991	1991	2000	2009					1985	1985			2003									1988
0.71			1990	1989	1999	2008					1984	1984			2001									1986
0.70			1988	1983	1997						1983	1984			2000		2010							1985
0.69			1987		1996						1982	1983			1999		2009							1983
0.68			1985		1994						1981	1982		**2005**	1998		2009							1981
0.67			1984		1993						1980	1982		2003	1997		2008							
0.66			1982		1991							1981		2002	1996		2007							
0.65			1981		1990							1980	2007	2001	1995		2006							
0.64					1988								2007	2000	1994		2005							
0.63					1987								**2008**	1999	1993		2004							
0.62					1986								2002	1998	1992	**2012**	2003							
0.61					1984								2001	1997	1991	1999	2002							
0.60					1983								1999	1997	1990	1998	2002							
0.59					1982								1998	1996	1989	1997	2001							
0.58					1981								1996	1995	1989	1996	2000							
0.57													1995	1994	1988	1996	1999	**2009**						
0.56													1993	1994	1988	1995	1998	2009						
0.55													1992	1993	1987	1994	1997	2008						
0.54													1991	1992	1987	1993	1997	2008						
0.53													1989	1991	1986	1992	1996							
0.52													1987	1991	1985	1992	1995							
0.51													1984	1990	1985	1991	1994							
0.50													1982	1989	1984	1990	1993							
0.49													1980	1988	1983	1987	1992							
0.48														1988	1983	1985	1991							
0.47														1987	1982	1982	1991							
0.46														1986	1982	1980	1990							
0.45														1986	1981		1989							
0.44														1985	1980		1988							
0.43														1984			1987							
0.42														1984			1987							
0.41														1983			1986							
0.40														1982			1985							
0.39														1982			1984							
0.38														1981			1984							
0.37														1980			1983							
0.36																	1982							
0.35																	1981							
0.34																	1981							

FIGURE 20 A quick visual overview of trends 1980-2012 for Gulf Coordination countries: time when a given indicator level was attained

SOURCE: Own calculations based on data from UNDP (2013b).

Chapter 9

CONCLUSIONS

1. There are two major lines of conclusions from this analysis of inequalities in the world in the human development index. In the broader horizon the first line of conclusions deals with the innovation that goes beyond the present state-of-the art in measuring the degree of inequality. Well-being and development are multidimensional and long-term phenomena; people compare and assess their positions over many dimensions and over time. The theoretical concept of time distance dimension of inequality and the two novel statistical measures S-time-distance and S-time-step present a very useful approach to complement (not replace) the existing mostly static measures of inequality in many fields. The new generic time distance approach offers a new view of existing data that is exceptionally easy to understand and to communicate, and it allows for developing and exploring new hypotheses and perspectives.

2. The second line of conclusions deals with the new insights that application of the time distance framework brings to the perception of the degree of inequality in the HDI and the consequences for the strategic considerations in preparations for the post-2015 era. The statistical results indicated that for the HDI (and also for life expectancy) the static differences in percentage terms in many cases appear to be small, while the time distance dimension gives a very different perception of the magnitude of the gap. S-time-distance measure gives a rough impression of the magnitude of world inequality by indicating a perception of a larger degree of disparity from the time dimension perspective than the respective percentage measure. For the past the time distances between the very high and the low HD group of about 74 years for non-income HDI, about 82 years for HDI and about 100 years for income index are relevant statistical descriptive measures of the situation easily understandable by everyone, balancing the static view. This additional insight provides a signal to politicians about the severity of the challenge at the starting point of formulating and deciding on the post-2015 agenda as well as the degree of urgency to tackle inequalities between and within countries.

3. The published UNDP data trends of the HDI and component indices (1980-2012) make the application of the broader dynamic time distance methodology possible. We are taking these data as input into the time distance analysis and showing what seeing the HDI data with new eyes can add to the understanding and perception of the degree of inequalities in the world. In preparing policy decisions other information and considerations need to be taken into account but the time distance concept and the methodological tools provided here can be utilised also in such enlarged frameworks.

4. Chapter 2 serves two purposes. On the one hand, it discusses the salient features of the

49

time distance concept and methodology presenting this innovative approach for looking at time-series data and in this context providing new statistical measures to discuss and evaluate the degree of inequality. Their definition is complemented with the time matrix format of presentation and visualising data over many units and over time as well as using this format as one of the approaches to calculate values of the S-time-distance and the S-time-step measures. S-time-distance measures the gap in time when two compared countries achieved the same level of HDI (for example, the HDI level of 0.55 was attained in China in 1996, in India in 2011, the latter lagging in time 15 years). On the other hand, the empirical examples using life expectancy as the example provide also important substantive conclusions of inequalities in this important indicator of well-being and development.

5. The levels of life expectancy experienced in the period 1980-2012 for 13 selected countries from the whole range of HDI from Norway (rank 1) to Niger (rank 186) were displayed in the table-graph format of time matrix in Figure 2. It was immediately visually clear that the trends for countries were so far apart that in the observed period of 32 years the 1980 level for Norway could be found in the latest years only in about the first 50 countries out of the 187 countries. So from the UNDP 2013 Report data the values of S-time-distance, which requires that the compared units reach the same level of the indicator, could be calculated only for a restricted number of countries. Therefore, the long-term trend of life expectancy for Sweden from Mitchell (2003) was introduced as the benchmark trend, which allowed the calculation of time lead and lag in life expectancy for all countries to provide a perception of the magnitude of inequalities in the time distance dimension for life expectancy.

6. For 2012 level of life expectancy for Niger one has to go back in the history of Sweden to find that level in year 1905, indicating the S-time-distance of about 107 years. For the recent levels of life expectancy for the selected countries the degree of disparity in time behind benchmark Sweden was very high, for Uruguay and Argentina about 24 and 30 years, for Turkey and Tunisia about 43 and 46 years, around 50 years for China, around 65 for Indonesia and Bangladesh, between 70 and 72 years for Kenya, Pakistan and India, for Niger more than 100 years. This is a new way to assess the reality by applying the novel statistical methodology. In an earlier study Sicherl (2012) e.g. about three quarters of the countries of the low HD group were for life expectancy lagging benchmark Sweden between 90 and 130 years, which confirms these conclusions.

7. The life expectancy analysis confirmed the theoretical proposition that perceptions of the size of the gap in life expectancy can be very different depending on the statistical measure used. The static difference against Sweden showed that it was lower for 10 percent for China and 11 percent for Lithuania (which may appear to be small) while the time distance was around 50 and 55 years, respectively (which gives a very different perception of the magnitude of the gap). This will be observed also in Chapter 3 for the gaps in the two dimensions for HDI.

Another observation was established for S-time-step as an additional measure of dynamics. It is very easy to understand, for 1 year of increase in life expectancy in the very high group about 5.5 years were needed, for the low group about 2.5 years were needed for 1 year of increase in life expectancy at much lower level. Both measures, conventional percentage growth rate and S-time-step, are valid description of the dynamics of change.

8. Comparing trends in HDI for four HD groups and also for the 13 selected countries in Chapter 3 showed that the largest gaps and largest time distances were in income index, the gaps in non-income HDI were considerably less. The range of HDI values over the three decades was 0.18 - 0.95. Again, there were substantial improvements in these selected countries in HDI in the analysed period but disparities remain very high between the four HD groups as indicated in conclusion 2 above. Between the selected countries we used China (which was one the best performers) as an interesting benchmark to which other countries are compared. China was still nearly 24 years behind Argentina at the lower end of the very high human development group; in turn Argentina is about 30 years behind the leading countries like Norway and Australia. China was ahead of Bangladesh for 19 years, for Pakistan 18 years, and for India 15 years. About 15 countries of the low group have still not reached the level of China in 1980.

9. In Chapter 4 Figure 8 shows the world view over four HD groups and four indices (HDI and the three component indices). In the time matrix one can compare in two directions: comparing between the four groups - very high (VHHD), high (HHD), medium (MHD), and low (LHD) group - for a given index and/or comparing the four indices within any given HD group. In general health index is the highest component attained, followed by education and income (for MHD in LHD groups income is higher than education). Looking at time distances between the HD groups there are interesting differences between the four indices. For the overall HDI the time distances between the HD groups are more than 32 years, 25 years, and 23 years, respectively. The smallest time distances for the components are those for education index. For education index the time distances between the HD groups are 26 years, 21 years, and 22 years. For health index the time distances between the HD groups are more than 32 years, 12 years, and more than 32 years. For income index the respective time distances between the HD groups are the largest, showing the large gaps in income levels and large time distances.

10. Comparing the three indices within each HD groups the time distances between the levels of the three indices for averages were for very high group (VHHD) much smaller than for other groups. The level of health index is the highest, the level of education index is lagging behind the level of health index for 9 years and that of income index at the lower level for 22 years; the time lag of income index behind education index is low (5 years).

Across the three component indices the fastest dynamics is shown for the education index where the S-time-step indicates that about 1.4 years were in the past needed for the increase of one level of the index (0.1). The dynamics of the health index was slower as it was needed between 2.3 and 3 years for one unit of increase on the average over the period. While past performance should not be simply extrapolated into the future, S-time-step can provide a hint how fast higher levels of indices could be achieved in a more simple understandable terms than when dynamics is expressed in percentage terms, which very much depend on the starting levels.

11. Chapter 5 gives an overview over all 187 countries showing time distance inequalities between countries within each of the four human development groups from the respective HDI average for the group (for levels that were attained in the period 1980-2012 in each of the groups). HDI time matrices for all four HD groups and the respective matrices of S-time-step are too large to be adequately presented in the book. Therefore, only four matrices of the S-time-distances showing time distance inequalities within each group are presented here, which can be also a rich source of information of comparison between countries depending on the interest of the user. The general conclusion is that the disparities in HDI are also large within the analysed HD groups.

12. For the very high HD group we can approximately say for the range between the Norway and Croatia that HDI for Croatia is about 16 percent lower and Croatia is lagging behind Norway for about 32 years. The within group inequalities in the HHD group are lower than in the VHHD group; the range between the Bahrain and Tunisia shows that HDI for Tunisia is about 11 percent lower and Tunisia is lagging behind Bahrain for about 22 years. In the medium group Cambodia, Lao, Swaziland, and Bhutan are lagging behind the group average for about 13 years which is considerably less than the time lag for the lowest countries in the very high and in the low group. The low group shows considerable larger intra-group inequalities.

13. Average value of HDI for the high (HHD) development group is the percentage terms about 16 percent lower than that of the very high group (VHHD), while the time distance has been more than 32 years, which is indicating a rather long period of time when there was no similarity in the level of the HDI. If we approximate the degree of inequality between Norway and Niger, in percentage terms Niger has about 32 percent of Norway and in time distance dimension the degree of inequality is approximated by the time delay of more than 104 years.

It seems that we can conclude in the same way as it was shown for the inequalities in the life expectancy that also for the HDI the static differences in percentage terms in many cases appear to be small, while the time distance dimension gives a very different perception of the magnitude of the gap; a very important conclusion for a more realistic perception of reality.

14. As indicated earlier the time matrix format of the HDI results for four HD groups (which are too large to be easily presented in the book) will be provided in the electronic form at the Gaptimer web page (link is available in Appendix A2) so that everybody can select any number of countries for comparisons depending on the interest of the user. Here we show such visualisation and possible comparisons for three examples: in Chapter 6 the HDI situation between EU27 countries and among five neighbouring countries in Central Europe; in Chapter 7 between the five BRICS countries comprising about 43 percent of the world population; and in Chapter 8 between six countries of the Gulf Coordination Council.

15. EU27 countries, with the exception of Bulgaria and Romania, belong to the very high HD group. The largest difference is between Netherlands and Bulgaria, the absolute difference in HDI is 0.139, in percentage terms Bulgaria is 15.1 percent lower than Netherlands, and the time distance was more than 32 years. For non-income HDI the best five EU27 countries occupied high positions in the world table: Ireland rank 4, Germany rank 7, Netherlands rank 8, Sweden rank 12, and Slovenia rank 13. The between countries example is provided of the HDI position of five EU countries, i.e. Slovenia and four neighbouring countries, Austria, Italy, Hungary, and Croatia. Between the five countries for HDI the leading country was Austria, behind it Slovenia with a lag of two years, Italy 5 years, Hungary about 15 years and Croatia about 20 years. It is interesting that by component indices there were cases where some of these countries are better that the average for the very high HD group: for the health index Italy had a time lead of about 10 years and Austria of 5 years, for education index Slovenia was about 8 years ahead, and for income index Austria with the time lead of about 7 years.

16. The BRICS countries occupied, with respect to the world rank for HDI in 2012: Russia rank 55, Brazil rank 85 (both in high HD group), China rank 101, South Africa rank 121, and India rank 136 (all three in medium HD group). The S-time-distances amounted to 10 years of time lag of Brazil behind Russia, 6 years of China behind of Brazil, 7 years of South Africa behind China, and more than 32 years of India behind South Africa. The value of the health index is highest in Brazil and China, followed by Russia, India, and South Africa. Brazil was ahead of Russia for 14 years, and ahead of India for 24 years; the present value of health index for South Africa was much lower than in any other BRICS country.

17. Russia was very much ahead of all other four countries in education index. It was followed by South Africa, Brazil, and China with a great delay for India; although there was substantial progress in attaining higher values of index over the period in all countries. Russia had the highest level of income index followed by Brazil and South Africa and a slightly lower level for China. Russia is about 8 years ahead of Brazil and South Africa, and more ahead of China which is growing very fast. The level of India is much lower, about 30 percent below the level of Russia. The highest dynamics in general was that in the education index (average of S-time-step about 1.2 years) followed by the income index (average 1.4 years with large deviations) and slower dynamics in health index. Within countries, dynamics for China was exceptional for income index, average for education index, and slow for health index. BRICS countries show with very interesting differences both with respect to levels across the component indices as well as their dynamics as presented by S-time-step statistics.

18. The six countries belong to two HD groups: Qatar and United Arab Emirates (UAE) to the very high, while Bahrain, Kuwait, Saudi Arabia, and Oman to the high HD group. The respective ranks in the world HDI rankings were in 2012 36, 41, for the first two countries, and 48, 54, 57, and 84 for others. The main characteristic of the time matrix for GCC countries shows that the highest values for three countries (Qatar, Kuwait, and UAE) are for income index, followed by health index, the lowest values for all six countries are for education index. For income index the three countries occupy very prominent ranks in the world rankings: Qatar rank 1, Kuwait 3, and UAE 10. However, for four of the GCC countries the income index decreased during the analysed period.

19. The time matrices presenting visualisation of the development in the analysed period 1980-2012 for the HDI and three component indices for the four HD groups, for five Central European countries, for six BRICS countries, and for six GCC countries, showed different ordering of the level and the dynamics of the three HDI component indices. This means that even this decomposition into three sub-indices can indicate substantial differences in the structure of development. Another set of rich information for the 187 countries is provided in Excel format of time matrices for HDI for the four HD groups and of the respective matrices for S-time-step at the www.gaptimer.eu (link is available in Appendix A2).

20. This could enable everybody to use time distance method for analysing the time dimension of the degree of inequality in HDI without the need to calculate these values and prepare the visualisation via time matrix for combination of any group of country comparisons. The examples and conclusions of this Gaptimer Report No. 1 could be of assistance for such activities. There are two summary messages.

The new generic time distance approach, which is easy to understand and to communicate, offers a new view of reality that significantly complements existing mostly static measures of inequality in many fields. These additional insights have also a transparent matter-of-fact message to politicians and the international community about the degree of urgency to tackle wide inequalities between and within countries in formulating and deciding on the post-2015 agenda. Half-hearted business as usual will not do in view of the established magnitudes of the time dimension of inequalities.

REFERENCES

Eurostat (2006), Life expectancy by sex and age [mlexpec]. Accessed January 3, 2006.

Eurostat (2013), Life expectancy by age and sex [demo_mlexpec]. Accessed July 22, 2013.

Granger C.W.J., Jeon Y. (1997), Measuring Lag Structure in Forecasting Models – The Introduction of Time Distance, Discussion Paper 97–24, University of California, San Diego.

Granger C.W.J., Jeon Y. (2003), A time-distance criterion for evaluating forecasting models, International Journal of Forecasting, Vol. 19.

Klugman, J., Rodriguez, F., Choi, H.-J. (2011), The HDI 2010: New Controversies, Old Critiques, Research Paper 2011/1, UNDP, New York.

Maddison, A. (2010), Statistics on World Population, GDP and Per Capita GDP, 1–2008 AD; http://www.ggdc.net/MADDISON/oriindex.htm.

Mitchell, B.R. (2003), International Historical Statistics, Europe 1750-2000, Fifth Edition. Palgrave, Macmillan, New York.

OECD (2013), Development Co-operation Report 2013: Ending Poverty, OECD Publishing. http://dx.doi.org/10.1787/dcr-2013-en

Sicherl, P. (1973), Time Distance as a Dynamic Measure of Disparities in Social and Economic Development, Kyklos, XXVI, Fasc. 3.

Sicherl, P. (1992), "Integrating Comparisons Across Time and Space: Methodology and Applications to Disparities within Yugoslavia", Journal of Public Policy 12, 4.

Sicherl, P. (1993), Integrating Comparisons Across Time And Space, Methodology and Applications to Disparities within Yugoslavia, Studies in Public Policy, No 213. Centre for the Study of Public Policy, University of Strathclyde, Glasgow.

Sicherl, P. (1999), "A New View in Comparative Analysis", IB Revija, 1/1999, Ljubljana.

Sicherl, P. (2007), "The inter-temporal aspect of well-being and societal progress", Social Indicators Research 84: 231–247.

Sicherl, P. (2011a), "New Understanding and Insights from Time-Series Data Based on Two Generic Measures: S-Time-Distance and S-Time-Step", OECD Statistics Working Papers, 2011/09. OECD Publishing, Paris. http://dx.doi.org/10.1787/5kg1zpzzl1tg-en

Sicherl, P. (2011b), Visualization of 50 years of OECD countries at a glance, SICENTER, Ljubljana. http://www.gaptimer.eu/images/stories/texts/50%20years%20of%20OECD%20countries%20at%20a%20glance.pdf, http://www.wikiprogress.org/index.php/Visualisation_of_50_years_of_OECD_countries_at_a_glance

Sicherl, P. (2012), Time Distance in Economics and Statistics, New Insights from Existing Data. Edition echoraum, Wien.

Sicherl, P. (2013a), A geek's guide to measuring the MDGs, Guardian Professional, The Guardian, Friday 1 March 2013 12.48 GMT, web page
http://www.guardian.co.uk/global-development-professionals-network/2013/feb/28/measuring-mdgs.

Sicherl, P. (2013b), Gender differences in life expectancy in the EU, IB Revija, XLVII, 2/2013.

Sicherl, P. (in press), Inter-Temporal Aspect of Wellbeing. In A. C. Michalos (Ed.), Encyclopedia of Quality of Life and Well-Being Research. Dordrecht, Netherlands: Springer.

Sustainable Development Solutions Network (2013), An Action Agenda for Sustainable Development, Report for the UN Secretary-General, www.unsdsn.org.

UNDP (2013a), Human Development Report 2013, The Rise of the South: Human Progress in a Diverse World, New York.

UNDP (2013b), UNDP web page. Accessed June 6, 2013.
http://hdrstats.undp.org/en/tables/

UN (2013), A New Global Partnership: Eradicate Poverty and Transform Economies Through Sustainable Development. The Report of the High-Level Panel of Eminent Persons on the Post-2015 Development Agenda, New York.

LIST OF FIGURES AND TABLES

Figures

FIGURE 1 Gender disparities in life expectancy at birth, EU27 average in 2010: static index and time distance 9

FIGURE 2 Time matrix for life expectancy at birth for selected countries and for benchmark Sweden 12

FIGURE 3 S-time-distances (in years) indicating lag or lead behind the benchmark of long-term trend for Sweden 14

FIGURE 4 S-time-step (in years) as an additional measure of dynamics of life expectancy - how many years were needed to reach the next level of the indicator 16

FIGURE 5 A quick visual overview over the four HD groups (trends 1980-2012) 20

FIGURE 6 A quick visual overview of HDI over selected countries (trends 1980-2012) 22

FIGURE 7 S-time-distance in years as a time measure of the gap, (-) time lead, (+) time lag from benchmark China for a given level of HDI 23

FIGURE 8 The world view over 4 HD groups and 4 indices (trends 1980-2012) 26

FIGURE 9 S-time-step: how many years were needed to reach the next level of the indicator, A quick visual overview of dynamics over all human development groups (trends 1980-2012) 28

FIGURE 10 S-time-distance in years as a time measure of the gap of countries from the very high human development group average for a given level of the HDI 30

FIGURE 11 S-time-distance in years as a time measure of the gap of countries from the high human development group average for a given level of the HDI 31

FIGURE 12 S-time-distance in years as a time measure of the gap of countries from the medium human development group average for a given level of the HDI 32

FIGURE 13 S-time-distance in years as a time measure of the gap of countries from the low human development group average for a given level of the HDI 33

FIGURE 14 Time matrix for HDI for EU27 countries (1980-2012) 37

FIGURE 15 S-time-distance in years as a time measure of the gap of EU27 countries from very high human development group (VHHD) 38

FIGURE 16 A quick visual overview of trends 1980-2012 for five Central European countries, Time matrix: time when a given indicator level was attained 40

FIGURE 17 S-time-distance in years as a time measure of the gap from average of the very high HD group as the benchmark 41

FIGURE 18 A quick visual overview over BRICS countries (trends 1980-2012), Time matrix: time when a given indicator level was attained 44

FIGURE 19 A quick visual overview over BRICS countries (trends 1980-2012), S-time-step: how many years were needed to reach the next level of the indicator 45

FIGURE 20 A quick visual overview of trends 1980-2012 for Gulf Coordination countries, Time matrix: time when a given indicator level was attained 48

Tables

TABLE 1 The perception of the magnitude of the differences in life expectancy may differ depending on the measure used 15

TABLE 2 Different perception of inequality based on percentage and time distance measures for HDI 34

APPENDIX
-
ELECTRONIC SUPPLEMENTARY MATERIAL

A1 Methodology

For methodology see freely available paper by Statistics Directorate, OECD:
P. Sicherl, New Understanding and Insights from Time-Series Data Based on Two Generic
Measures: S-time-distance and S-time-step; Working paper No. 44, Statistics Directorate, OECD
Publishing, Paris, November 2011.
Please download the paper on http://dx.doi.org/10.1787/5kg1zpzzl1tg-en.

More detailed methodological issues and numerous applications are available in the book:
Pavle Sicherl, Time Distance in Economics and Statistics, New Insights from Existing Data,
p. 444, Echoraum, Vienna, 2012.
More information is available on wikiprogress
http://www.wikiprogress.org/index.php/Time_Distance_in_Economics_and_Statistics

The book is available on amazon.de
http://www.amazon.de/gp/product/3901941274

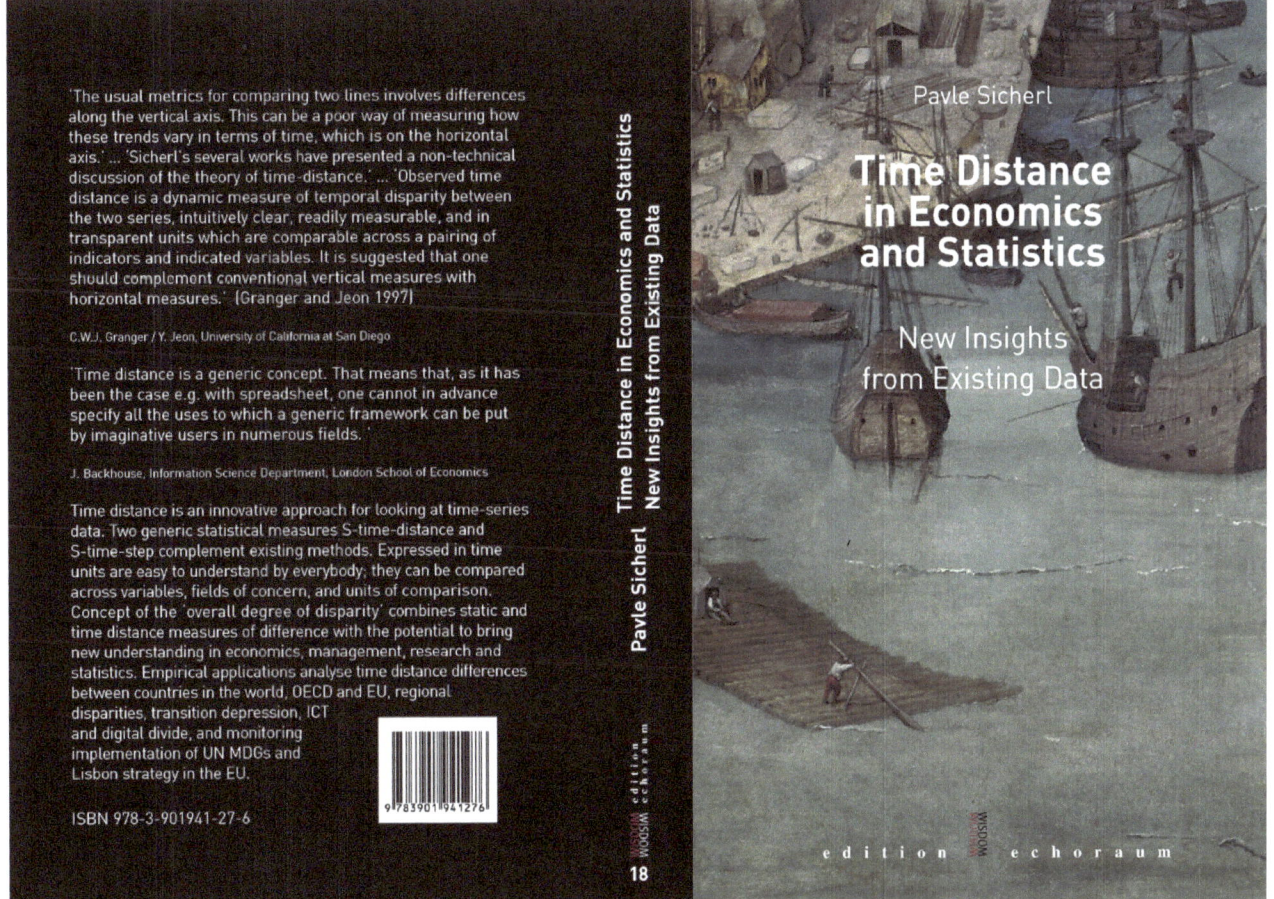

A2 More detailed HDI time matrices and S-time-step calculations for 187 countries

The Figures 10-13 present the important overview in terms of time distance inequalities within each group. The general conclusion is that the disparities in HDI are also large within the analysed groups. These figures and the electronic supplementary files can be also a rich source of information of comparison between countries of users' interest.

Time matrices for all four HD groups and the respective matrices of S-time-step are too large to be adequately presented in the book. However, these results can be obtained in the electronic form.

Following Excel files, very useful for users for presentation and/or for further calculations, are available for download at www.gaptimer.eu/esm1.zip.

Time matrices:
Time matrix for HDI for very high human development group.xls
Time matrix for HDI for high human development group.xls
Time matrix for HDI for medium human development group.xls
Time matrix for HDI for low human development group.xls

S-time-step tables:
S-time-step for HDI for very high human development group.xls
S-time-step for HDI for high human development group.xls
S-time-step for HDI for medium human development group.xls
S-time-step for HDI for low human development group.xls

INDEX

methodology,
3, 7, 8, 11, 15, 17, 49, 50, 59
different perception of inequality,
33
inequalities,
7, 8, 9, 11, 14, 15, 17, 19, 21, 25, 29, 30, 31, 32, 33, 35, 49, 50, 52, 54, 59
gender inequality in life expectancy,
9, 10,
trends in world inequalities in HDI,
19, 20, 22
overall Human Development Index, health, education, and income components,
25
overview over 187 countries,
29
disparities within EU27,
8, 9, 37, 38, 39, 52, 53
BRICS countries,
8, 43, 44, 45, 46, 47, 53, 54, 60
GCC countries,
47, 48, 54

Human Development Index,
7, 19, 20, 21, 22, 23, 25, 26, 28, 30, 31, 32, 33, 37, 38, 40, 41, 44, 45, 48, 60
non-income HDI,
19, 20, 21, 25, 39, 49, 51
health index,
7, 11, 17, 19, 25, 27, 39, 40, 41, 43, 46, 47, 51, 53, 54

education index,
7, 19, 25, 27, 39, 40, 41, 43, 46, 47, 51, 53, 54
income index,
7, 19, 21, 25, 27, 39, 40, 41, 43, 45, 46, 47, 49, 51, 53, 54
life expectancy,
8, 9, 10, 11, 12, 13, 14, 15, 16, 17, 21, 33, 35, 49, 50, 52, 55
S-time-distance,
7, 8, 10, 13, 14, 15, 16, 17, 18, 21, 23, 25, 29, 30, 31, 32, 33, 34, 38, 39, 40, 41, 43, 49, 50, 52, 53, 59, 64
S-time-step,
6, 7, 10, 13, 16, 17, 18, 27, 28, 29, 34, 37, 43, 45, 46, 47, 49, 50, 51, 52, 53, 54, 59, 60
time matrix,
11, 13, 14, 15, 18, 19, 23, 25, 37, 39, 47, 50, 51, 52, 54
electronic supplementary material,
8, 59

low human development group,
15, 16, 21, 23, 25, 27, 31, 32, 33, 34, 35, 49, 50, 51, 52, 59
medium human development group,
15, 16, 21, 25, 27, 31, 32, 34, 43, 46, 52, 53, 59
high human development group,
10, 15, 16, 21, 23, 25, 27, 30, 31, 34, 35, 38, 39, 40, 43, 46, 47, 53, 51, 59
very high human development group,
10, 15, 16, 21, 23, 27, 29, 30, 34, 35, 38, 39, 40, 41, 51, 52, 53, 59

Index for 187 Countries

Pages for countries in **bold** refer to figures and tables, others to the text.

A

Afghanistan, **33**
Albania, **31**
Algeria, **31,** 30
Andorra, **30**
Angola, **33**
Antigua and Barbuda, **31**
Argentina, **12, 14, 22, 23, 30,** 15, 23, 29, 35, 50, 51
Armenia, **31**
Australia, **12, 14, 22, 23, 30,** 13, 15, 23, 29, 37, 51
Austria, **30, 37, 38, 40, 41, 60,** 38, 39, 40, 41, 53
Azerbaijan, **31**

B

Bahamas, **31**

Bahrain, **31, 34, 48,** 30, 47, 52, 53
Bangladesh, **12, 14, 22, 23, 33,** 13, 15, 23, 50, 51
Barbados, **30**
Belarus, **31**
Belgium, **30, 37, 38,** 38, 39
Belize, **32,** 31
Benin, **33**
Bhutan, **32, 34,** 31, 52
Bolivia (Plurinational State of), **32**
Bosnia and Herzegovina, **31**
Botswana, **32**
Brazil, **31, 44, 45,** 43, 45, 46, 53
Brunei Darussalam, **30**
Bulgaria, **31, 37, 38,** 37, 39, 53
Burkina Faso, **33**

Burundi, **33**

C

Cambodia, **32,** 31, 52
Cameroon, **33**
Canada, **30,** 29
Cape Verde, **32**
Central African Republic, **33**
Chad, **33**
Chile, **30**
China, **12, 14, 15, 22, 23, 32, 34, 44, 45,** 8, 10, 15, 19, 23, 27, 35, 43, 45, 46, 50, 51, 53, 57
Colombia, **31**
Comoros, **33**
Congo, **33, 34,** 32, 35
Congo (Democratic Republic of the), **33**
Costa Rica, **31**
Côte d'Ivoire, **33,** 32
Croatia, **30, 34, 40, 41, 60,** 29, 35, 39, 40, 41, 52, 53
Cuba, **31**
Cyprus, **30, 37, 38**
Czech Republic, **30, 37, 38**

D

Denmark, **30, 37, 38,** 38, 39
Djibouti, **33**
Dominica, **31**
Dominican Republic, **32,** 31

E

Ecuador, **31**
Egypt, **32**
El Salvador, **32**
Equatorial Guinea, **32**
Eritrea, **33**
Estonia, **30, 37, 38**
Ethiopia, **33,** 64

F

Fiji, **32**
Finland, **30, 37, 38,** 39
France, **30, 37, 38,** 38, 39

G

Gabon, **32**
Gambia, **33**
Georgia, **31**
Germany, **30, 37, 38,** 38, 39, 53
Ghana, **32**
Greece, **30, 37, 38**
Grenada, **31**
Guatemala, **32**
Guinea, **33**
Guinea-Bissau, **33**
Guyana, **32**

H

Haiti, **33,** 32

Honduras, **32**
Hong Kong, China (SAR), **30**
Hungary, **30, 37, 38, 40, 41, 60,** 39, 40, 41, 53

I

Iceland, **30**
India, **12, 14, 22, 23, 32, 44, 45,** 10, 15, 19, 23, 43, 46, 50, 51, 53
Indonesia, **12, 14, 22, 23, 32,** 15, 50
Iran (Islamic Republic of), **31**
Iraq, **32**
Ireland, **30, 37, 38,** 38, 39, 53
Israel, **30**
Italy, **30, 37, 38, 40, 41, 60,** 39, 40, 41, 53

J

Jamaica, **31**
Japan, **30**
Jordan, **32**

K

Kazakhstan, **31**
Kenya, **12, 14, 22, 23, 33,** 15, 32, 50
Kiribati, **32**
Korea (Republic of), **30**
Kuwait, **31, 48,** 30, 47, 53
Kyrgyzstan, **32**

L

Lao People's Democratic Republic, **32**
Latvia, **30, 37, 38,** 29, 38
Lebanon, **31**
Lesotho, **33**
Liberia, **33**
Libya, **31**
Liechtenstein, **30**
Lithuania, **15, 30, 37, 38,** 15, 50
Luxembourg, **30, 37, 38**

M

Madagascar, **33**
Malawi, **33**
Malaysia, **31**
Maldives, **32**
Mali, **33**
Malta, **30, 37, 38**
Mauritania, **33**
Mauritius, **31**
Mexico, **31**
Micronesia (Federated States of), **32**
Moldova (Republic of), **32**
Mongolia, **32**
Montenegro, **31**
Morocco, **32**
Mozambique, **33**
Myanmar, **33**

N

Namibia, **32**
Nepal, **33,** 35
Netherlands, **30, 37, 38,** 37, 38, 39, 53, 56
New Zealand, **30**
Nicaragua, **32**
Niger, **12, 14, 15, 22, 23, 33, 34,** 13, 14, 15, 16, 25, 32, 35, 50, 52
Nigeria, **33**
Norway, **12, 14, 22, 23, 30, 34,** 13, 15, 23, 25, 29, 35, 37, 50, 51, 52

O

Oman, **31, 48,** 47, 53

P

Pakistan, **12, 14, 22, 23, 33,** 13, 15, 23, 50, 51
Palau, **31**
Palestine, State of, **32**
Panama, **31**
Papua New Guinea, **33**
Paraguay, **32**
Peru, **31**
Philippines, **32**
Poland, **30, 37, 38**
Portugal, **30, 37, 38**

Q

Qatar, **30, 48,** 47, 53

R

Romania, **31, 37, 38,** 38, 39, 53
Russian Federation, **31, 44, 45,** 43, 45, 46, 53
Rwanda, **33**

S

Saint Kitts and Nevis, **31**
Saint Lucia, **31**
Saint Vincent and the Grenadines, **31**
Samoa, **32**
Sao Tome and Principe, **33**
Saudi Arabia, **31, 48,** 47, 53
Senegal, **33**
Serbia, **31**
Seychelles, **30,** 29
Sierra Leone, **33**
Singapore, **30**
Slovakia, **30, 37, 38**
Slovenia, **30, 37, 38, 40, 41, 60,** 38, 39, 40, 41, 53, 64
Solomon Islands, **33**
South Africa, **32, 44, 45,** 31, 43, 45, 46, 53
Spain, **30, 37, 38**
Sri Lanka, **31,** 30
Sudan, **33**
Suriname, **32**
Swaziland, **32,** 31, 52
Sweden, **12, 14, 15, 30, 37, 38,** 8, 11, 12, 13, 14, 15, 21, 29, 35, 38, 39, 50, 53, 57
Switzerland, **30,** 29

Syrian Arab Republic, **32**

T

Tajikistan, **32**
Tanzania (United Republic of), **33**
Thailand, **32**
The former Yugoslav Republic of Macedonia, **31**
Timor-Leste, **32**
Togo, **33,** 32
Tonga, **32**
Trinidad and Tobago, **31**
Tunisia, **12, 14, 22, 23, 31,** 13, 15, 30, 50, 52
Turkey, **12, 14, 22, 23, 31,** 13, 15, 23, 50
Turkmenistan, **32**

U

Uganda, **33**
Ukraine, **31**
United Arab Emirates, **30, 48,** 47, 53
United Kingdom, **30, 37, 38**
United States, **30,** 29, 37
Uruguay, **12, 14, 22, 23, 31,** 15, 50
Uzbekistan, **32**

V

Vanuatu, **32**
Venezuela (Bolivarian Republic of), **31**
Viet Nam, **32**

Y

Yemen, **33**

Z

Zambia, **33**
Zimbabwe, **33**

ABOUT THE AUTHOR

Professor Pavle Sicherl, Founder of SICENTER and principal researcher, 1993-present, Professor of Economics, University of Ljubljana, Slovenia (1975-2003); macroeconomic adviser in the Harvard University Development Advisory Service team in Ethiopia, (1970-1974); in 1960's Deputy Director of the Yugoslav Institute of Economic Research in Belgrade.

Born February 16, 1935 in Ljubljana, Slovenian citizen. Ph.D. (economics) and Dipl.Econ., University of Ljubljana; M.A. Development Economics (Williams College, MA, USA). Speciality: growth and inequality, he introduced a new statistical measure, S-time-distance, to amend the present methods of analysing time-series data and disparities in many fields.

For this idea he received many fellowships and invitations: Senior Fulbright Research Award (Yale), London School of Economics, Institute of World Economics (Kiel), Institute for Advanced Studies (Vienna), etc. Visiting professor abroad, project leader for international and national projects, and consultant to the World Bank, OECD, UN, ILO, UNIDO, INSTRAW, ITU, EUROCHAMBRES.

Biography: Who's Who in the World, Marquis, 1991-1992 ... 2013.

Website: www.gaptimer.eu

Email: pavle.sicherl@gaptimer.eu